LEADING LASTING CHANGE

I₂E₂

Jayne Felgen

CREATIVE
HEALTH CARE
MANAGEMENT

Printed and bound in the United States of America.
Second Printing: July 2009

12 11 10 09   5 4 3 2

ISBN-13: 978-1-886624-12-2 (pbk.)

Library of Congress Cataloging-in-Publication Data
Felgen, Jayne A.
   I$_2$E$_2$: leading lasting change / by Jayne Felgen.
   p. ; cm.
Includes bibliographical references.
1. Health services administration. 2. Organizational change.
I. Title. II. Title: I two e two.
[DNLM: 1. Organizational Innovation. 2. Patient Care
Management—organization & administration. W 84.7 F312i 2007]
RA971.F45 2007
362.1068—dc22

2006100502

For permission and ordering information, write to:

Creative Health Care Management, Inc.
5610 Rowland Road, Suite 100
Minneapolis, MN 55343-8905

CREATIVE
HEALTH CARE
MANAGEMENT

chcm@chcm.com
or call: 800.728.7766 or 952.854.9015
www.chcm.com

*In memory of my mother, Mary Lou Wurstner,
whose delight in the details, both the design and
the delivery, brought visions to life with great creativity,
style and effect.*

Table of Contents

Acknowledgements. . . . . *vii*

Introduction *1*

Part I: Philosophies of Effective Change *5*

   1 *Guiding Principles* *7*

Part II: Fundamentals of I_2E_2 . . . . *33*

   2 *The Benefits of I_2E_2* *35*

   3 *Linking the Vision to Elements of I_2E_2* . . .*43*

   4 *Everyday Applications* *67*

Part III: Reflection: The BIDMC Merger *85*

   5 *What Happened?* *87*

   6 *All Elements in Place* *101*

Part IV: I_2E_2 in Practice *119*

   7 *Asking the Right Questions* *121*

   8 *Implementing Large-Scale Change: Relationship-Based Care Scenario* *133*

   9 *Strategies for Sustaining Change* *161*

   Appendices. *175*

   References *179*

Acknowledgements

I am very grateful to the following colleagues, friends and family for their help in bringing this book to life:

Susan Smith and Marie Manthey, whose knowledge, wisdom and experienced eyes informed their helpful feedback.

Rosanne Rasso, whose enthusiasm for I_2E_2 was my encouragement for this book.

Colleen Person, whose immediate and continued application of I_2E_2 concepts validated its practical value.

Rebecca Smith, my writing partner, who was truly a gift to me in this process. She made a potentially painful process a productive, rewarding and fun experience.

Beth Beaty, my managing editor, who guided us all on the journey from idea to book.

Chris Bjork, our resources director, who kept us firmly grounded while contributing to the creative process.

Jay Monroe, whose artistic interpretation helped convey the meaning and intent of I_2E_2.

My family, whose love, belief and pride in my work affirms and propels me.

All those colleagues whose commitment to making lasting change in their organizations inspires me.

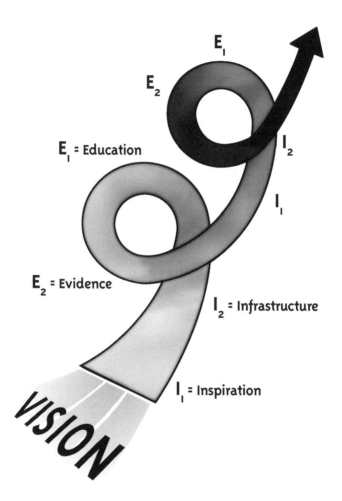

E₁
E₂
E₁ = Education
E₂ = Evidence
I₂
I₁
I₂ = Infrastructure
I₁ = Inspiration
VISION

Introduction

The Purpose of this Book

This book exists to help readers understand the fundamental elements of successful, large-scale change. It introduces a formula for change called I_2E_2 which helps users consider the broad scope of change in terms of four understandable elements: Inspiration (I_1), Infrastructure (I_2), Education (E_1) and Evidence (E_2). In every instance of successful, sustained change each of these elements is represented fully and tended to meticulously. It is my belief that even agents of successful change who are not familiar with the concept of I_2E_2 follow this formula intuitively without realizing it. My aim is to show readers how to put together an effective plan for leading and managing change using this elemental formula.

How to Use This Book

I_2E_2: Leading Lasting Change is designed to be used in different ways by different readers at different times.

This book has been divided into four parts—the first three explaining the concept itself as well as many of its possible applications, and a fourth describing exactly how leaders of large-scale change can use I_2E_2 to make their change initiatives comprehensive, inclusive and long-lasting.

Part I: Philosophies of Effective Change offers guiding principles to help prepare anyone embarking on large-scale change to stay focused on the very best of what his or her organization offers.

This is a brief section designed to help leaders at all levels manage their own mindsets before embarking on organization-wide change. Its overarching message is this: You can choose where you focus your attention—and it matters where you do. Readers may wish to return to this section frequently for inspiration over the course of a large-scale change.

Part II: Fundamentals of I_2E_2 introduces the benefits of using I_2E_2 to create action plans for change and explores the four elements of I_2E_2 in detail.

This section is especially helpful for anyone who will be in a position to teach the concepts of I_2E_2 to others, as it applies the elements of I_2E_2 to some of our simplest everyday tasks. The section includes three brief, bare-bones scenarios designed to help readers grasp the essence of I_2E_2. While some readers may find these scenarios simplistic, others will find that they provide welcome clarity as they show I_2E_2 in its most fundamental form.

Part III: Reflection: The Beth Israel Deaconess Medical Center (BIDMC) merger demonstrates that the elements of Inspiration (I_1), Infrastructure (I_2), Education (E_1) and Evidence (E_2) are always carefully tended to in any instance of successful change.

This section is essential reading for leaders responsible for managing cultural change, as it dissects the scenario of a large-scale change that was unsuccessful in its initial stages, though thoroughly successful in the end. By analyzing the two phases of the change with I_2E_2 in mind, we can see that carefully tending to each of the elements in I_2E_2 is fundamental to successful change.

Part IV: I_2E_2 in Practice offers a comprehensive application of I_2E_2 to the design and implementation of organization-wide change.

A large portion of the consulting we do at Creative Health Care Management (CHCM) involves bringing Relationship-Based Care (RBC) to health care organizations all over the world. For this reason I've included a chapter in which I_2E_2 is used to plan and manage the implementation of RBC. This section is essential reading for anyone leading change in an organization transitioning to RBC, but it will be equally helpful for those implementing any other organization-wide cultural change. It is also good information for a broader spectrum of individuals in organizations undergoing transformation (especially transformation to RBC), as it explains what goes into a comprehensive plan for change as well as the rationale behind it.

The Core Message Embedded in this Book

The first chapter of this book spotlights a philosophical framework that serves as the foundation of I_2E_2.

This framework and the related guiding principles will be described in detail at the outset and referred to throughout the book as they are applied in real-world scenarios. While their details are many and their explanations complete, their essence is simple:

If you keep your focus on what really matters—what is working and why it's working—your energy and that of those around you can be effectively deployed to get you more of it.

PART

I

Philosophies of
Effective Change

1

Guiding Principles

As a leader in the field of health care, I have occasion to speak to and interact with thousands of health care professionals in several countries each year. While I speak on many different topics, I have found that a few core philosophical assumptions have become pillars in my work. As I_2E_2 evolved, I soon discovered that not only are these core assumptions complementary to it; they're actually embedded in it.

While it will quickly become obvious to you that I_2E_2 can help us be organized and comprehensive, I want to make explicit at the outset the ways in which it also helps us to be influential, exuberant, abundant, appreciative, clearly focused, intentional and integral.

Effective leadership requires, first and foremost, managing your own mindset.

People do their best work when they think and act as their "best selves." Spending time considering the philosophies that follow (many of which will not be new to you) will help bring you into full alignment with your best self. These eight philosophical principles are explained in detail here and will reappear often throughout the text of this book.

I. Make Every Inquiry "Appreciative"

When an organization takes on a project to implement substantive change, often it is generally assumed that the reason the project is necessary is that things are not good enough just as they are. I'd like to weave into this common perception of organizational change, the thread of Appreciative Inquiry (Cooperrider & Srivastva, 1987).

It sometimes happens that when one group of individuals seeks change, the group who has put the current system into place suddenly finds itself associated with what is old, flawed or failing. Appreciative Inquiry helps us to be more respectful about what is already in place in the organization we wish to change.

If there is a system in place that is not working as well as it could be, there is also a person or group of people who put that system into place, and any one of those people might be seated next to you in the boardroom.

A practice of Appreciative Inquiry—the practice of looking at "what is" with appreciation for what it has provided for us so far—allows us to move forward unencumbered by the ghosts of past failures. Further, Appreciative Inquiry helps us to create our plans for change based more solidly on what we already know is effective, instead of positioning us to create *against* what we know we do not want. It is essentially a tool of perception—without Appreciative Inquiry, we may perceive barriers as immovable. But with our focus on what is working—and by extension, on what is possible—we feel empowered to remove the barriers we see in order to create the ease we want.

> **Appreciative Inquiry is a tool that helps enlighten us regarding past experiences in which we have achieved success about what matters most.**

With Appreciative Inquiry as our guide, we consistently convey the empowering message, "If you had the competence, commitment and integrity to do *that*, I'm confident that you can do *this* too."

As agents of change we are agents of hope. Appreciative Inquiry focuses us squarely on the information poised to give us the most tangible hope of all. It helps us to see our own past and current successes for what they really are: proof of our ability to achieve *future* success.

This book embraces the core assumption that looking with appreciation at what is already in place will help us get where we want to go much more effectively than looking for what is old, flawed or failing.

II. Use Your Influence

While the influence of highly placed leaders is usually obvious, anyone in an organization has the power to influence nearly anyone else. The question is this:

"Do we use our influence deliberately—or do we pay too little mind to the full scope of our influence?"

Positional leaders may wield the influence of the "bully pulpit", but the ability to deliver a mandate of any kind is the least valuable tool a leader has. No sustainable change comes about by mandate. Sustainable change comes through consensus building, heartfelt agreement and the sustained action of those committed to bringing the change to life and keeping it alive. All of these conditions are achieved by putting relationships first—and that goes for every relationship we have.

Consider for a moment how broadly we might define "relationship" in a context like this one. We have, of course, one-to-one relationships, but we can also look at the ways we relate to groups, the ways we relate to our readers in our written communications, the ways we relate to our physical environment and so on.

In every one of our relationships, we have influence—and if we are in leadership positions, we have substantial influence on others whether we influence them deliberately or not.

The power of influence has been written about perhaps most succinctly by Stephen Covey. In his work on influence, his primary focus is helping us understand what we can and cannot influence as well as what does and does not broaden the *scope* of our influence (Covey, 2004).

Covey states that we have two "circles" to consider: our circle of concern, which contains everything that affects us (our environment, the people in our lives—essentially everything around us)—and our circle of influence, which contains everything within our circle of concern that we can have some direct, visible effect on.

Covey tells us that we only work effectively *within* our circle of influence. It is beyond our ability to change the circumstances and events outside of our circle of influence, so our focus on them is socially and professionally paralyzing.

In order to have a clear picture of our circle of influence, we must first know what we can and cannot change.

In health care, we often cultivate that knowing by defining boundaries in terms of our own Responsibility, Authority and Accountability (R+A+A). In the R+A+A model, responsibility refers to the clear and specific allocation and acceptance of duties. Authority refers to the right to act and make decisions. And accountability refers to one's own accounting of how he or she has met an expectation. Everything within our own R+A+A falls within our circle of influence (Creative Health Care Management, 2003).

Covey uses his discussion of the circles of influence and concern to help us see how we can be proactive rather than reactive. Putting our attention on our circle of influence makes us proactive and putting our attention outside of our circle of influence makes us reactive. Proactive people tend to lead productive, exuberant lives; reactive people tend to lead lives marked by frustration and dissatisfaction.

Focusing outside of our circle of influence is focusing on circumstances and events that we are powerless to change.

Much naysaying and crabbiness come from the feeling of hopelessness we experience in situations or circumstances that we can't change—and it is essential to note that the *feeling* of hopelessness about changing what we can't change is born directly from our focus on that which we can't change. Here we will establish a theme that you will see throughout this book:

We can—and must—consciously choose where we focus our attention.

When things are not as we want them to be, we can focus on what we can't change and experience feelings of hopelessness and discontent, or we can focus on what we *can* change and experience the fullness of our power to act proactively in our lives and in the lives of those around us.

This concept has some pretty tangible implications. If you focus on what is outside of your circle of influence you will see your circle of influence shrink as you not only give your attention to something that depletes you, but you also neglect the things you actually *can* influence while your attention is elsewhere.

It may seem at first that a focus that *doesn't* reach beyond one's current circle of influence is self-limiting. It may seem counterintuitive that refraining from reaching outside of one's current scope of influence actually works toward broadening that scope. But because we are only *effective* within our own circle of influence, we can only experience success in that circle, and success breeds more success. Reaching out of our circle of influence into the realm of things that we are powerless to change is not the way to bring something into our current circle of influence.

> *Our circle of influence grows when we become a positively charged magnetic force within it.*

Another aim of this line of inquiry is to stretch our perception of *what* we can ultimately influence. If you were to do an exercise in which you listed all of the people, circumstances and events within your circle of influence, you would undoubtedly compile an incomplete list. With some coaching you could add to your list, but if you are the least bit proactive— meaning if you put any attention at all on your circle of influence—your circle of influence grows at a rate that would never allow you to catalog everything in it.

> *In reality we have far more influence than most of us realize and therefore far more influence than it ever occurs to us to use deliberately.*

Our deepest fear is not that we are inadequate.
Our deepest fear is that we are powerful beyond measure.
It is our light, not our darkness that most frightens us.
We ask ourselves, Who am I to be brilliant, gorgeous,
talented, fabulous? Actually, who are you not to be?
You are a child of God. Your playing small does not serve the
world. There is nothing enlightened about shrinking so that
other people won't feel insecure around you.
We are all meant to shine, as children do.
We were born to make manifest the glory of God
that is within us. It's not just in some of us; it's in everyone.
And as we let our own light shine, we unconsciously give
other people permission to do the same.
As we are liberated from our own fear,
our presence automatically liberates others.

—Marianne Williamson
*A Return To Love: Reflections on the Principles of
A Course in Miracles*

Instead we may become overwhelmed by multiple concerns when we focus on things outside of our circle of influence.

Discussion of the finer points of a concept like the "circle of influence" are helpful to understand, but it's important to remember that while we can influence circumstances and events around us, our primary influence is always on people.

Leading change means influencing people deliberately.

Effective leaders don't have to drag others along with them. Effective leaders know how to use their influence to create agreement in those they lead by appealing to the achievement of a greater good. Further, effective leaders are humbled by the scope of their influence and they tend to it with great care at all times and in all places.

This book embraces the core assumption that the influence we have as leaders is a sacred trust. It is ours to understand, grow and direct by the power of our own thoughtful focus.

III. Experience Exuberance

Kay Redfield Jamison's book *Exuberance: The Passion for Life* begins with a reference to an Anglican prayer which petitions God to "Watch now those who weep this day; Rest your weary ones; Soothe your suffering ones." As she wryly points out, "The joyous tend to be left to their own devices, the exuberant ones even more so" (Redfield Jamison, 2005).

> *Much like our former, somewhat reflexive, focus on addressing problems rather than appreciating and building on our current strengths, we may still tend to put the lion's share of our attention on soothing the sad, stuck and frustrated instead of deliberately harnessing the joyfully creative productivity of the exuberant among us.*

We tend to write off the exuberant ones as pie-in-the-sky idealists or "Pollyannas." They are easy to dismiss, in part because we know they will not suffer personally because of our dismissal of them. (If we drop the exuberant ones, they bounce.)

> *But we miss a golden opportunity when we fail to take seriously the exuberant creators among us.*

Their exuberance makes them fountains of ideas—some extraordinary, but many merely practical. Exuberance is not mania; it is an expression of the flow of positive energy through a human body. It is the energy that accompanies (and sometimes causes) the position of being actively *for* something rather than being positioned against its opposite.

We tend to think that some people are naturally exuberant and that for others exuberance is not possible. But it is my experience (as one who is frequently exuberant, but not always so) that exuberance is not *just* natural; it can also be learned and practiced. If one's practiced habit is to focus on what is working well and therefore to position one's self to work for what is wanted, one will often experience exuberance. If it is one's practiced habit to focus on what is not working well and therefore to position one's self to work against what is not wanted, one will rarely if ever experience exuberance.

Exuberance comes and goes; it comes with focus on what is wanted and it goes with focus on what is not.

Exuberance is a powerful force, and while we may imagine that the great power of exuberance lies in its ability to help us persuade others to see things our way, its greatest power may in fact be its ability to keep the exuberant ones themselves passionately focused on the task at hand. Emotional energies waver throughout the course of a long transformational project. When the project needs a shot of energy (*well* before anything actually becomes stalled) the exuberance of those leading the change can be reignited by a renewed focus on the group's past and current successes—from which it is only a small leap to deliberately focus on creating its desired future.

Be ever mindful of the power of exuberance. Train yourself to recognize it and to *always* express gratitude for it when you see it. And remember that even when the light of exuberance is not visible, it is never far away.

This book embraces the core assumption that exuberance is possible for everyone and that deliberately practicing exuberance is one of the most valuable gifts we can offer in any collaboration of which we are part.

IV. Believe in Your Abundance

In any circumstance in which people collaborate, there exists the risk that some collaborators will become protective of the information with which they work. Someone in data management, for example, may be reluctant to surrender his data to someone elsewhere in the organization who wishes to use that data to inspire change. He may fear becoming expendable if he is not the only person who has access to and understanding of his data. Holding a perspective of diminishment can derail creative collaboration. Encouraging people to *own* their own practice or performance does not mean encouraging them to be protective of it. It means inviting them into a new way of being and then empowering them to make decisions within the parameters of that new way. It means fostering independent excellence and the confidence and competence to create *interdependent* relationships.

> *I advocate embarking on any creatively*
> *collaborative venture with a core assumption*
> *of abundance.*

As the president of a consulting firm with a publishing division, I am sometimes involved in internal conversations about how much information to include in our books: "Will sharing *too much* in our books work against us? Could we be giving away our business?" Absolutely not. Sharing the work *is* our business! In the spirit of abundance, we believe it is impossible to share too much. In the spirit of abundance, we want to model generosity, proactive sharing of information and transparency in our assistance to potential and existing clients. We aspire to do whatever it takes to contribute to the growth and development of our colleagues and to improve and strengthen the work of health care.

> *In any sort of information exchange*
> *(especially when we are all on the same team!)*
> *the more we share, the more we all gain.*

One of the nuances of abundance theory holds that we are also best off assuming that others care as much about making things better as we do. In the spirit of abundance, we never assume that others are less committed than we are. Time spent worrying about the commitment level of others is time wasted; time spent complaining about anyone else's lack of commitment harms the project immeasurably.

Helen Keller said, "I am only one; but I am still one. I cannot do everything, but still I can do something. I will not refuse to do the something I can do." When individuals come together to work in teams—true teams, as opposed to "work groups"—they blend their talents and work together for a common purpose. They create a synergy among them that makes everyone's load lighter and everyone's work more effective. Embracing a core assumption of abundance—the assumption that it is best to contribute what one *can* contribute whenever possible—turns work groups into teams and co-workers into colleagues.

This book embraces the core assumption that everyone has something of value to offer. The practice of consistently offering all that we can offer is fundamental to any initiative for successful, sustainable change.

V. Be Clear

If we want people to follow us, we must be clear with them about where we want them to go.

Because so much in health care comes at us all at once—new information, new procedures, life-and-death emergencies—it can feel sometimes like we are living in chaos. It can feel like no matter what new initiatives we take on, things invariably get derailed as "life happens" all around us.

Our clarity of purpose makes each of us a voice of common sense in a chaotic world.

Conversely, if our stated purpose sounds earnest and heartfelt, but its details are not clearly spelled out to those we wish to bring along with us, even the most willing among us will not follow for long—if for no other reason than that they will not know how to.

Only when the details of our purpose are clearly organized can that purpose be clearly articulated.

It is essential that we create the time to get organized enough to construct a solid platform for others to stand on. Anything that's worth doing deserves time and attention to the details.

It is curious that there are two well-known aphorisms about *details* that seem to contradict each other completely. It has long been common in our colloquial speech to say that "the devil is in the details." The "devil" is known to make every little task difficult, and sometimes we see details as difficulties—perhaps even as actual obstacles to the creation of our plans. We may struggle to "fill in all the blanks" and then worry that we've missed something essential anyway. After all, in health care every detail is potentially of life-and-death importance.

Another view is the one that comes to us from acclaimed architect Mies van der Rohe. He said, "*God* is in the details." As you put together a plan for substantive organizational change, you are *creating*. "In the beginning" there is all that you find when you look with appreciation at the current state of your organization. Once you begin to add details, you see your creation come to life. These details, often beautifully and lovingly crafted, add clarity to your vision for change. It is your visible attention to detail, along with your clear articulation of how the contribution of each individual in your organization fits into your plan, that makes it *possible* for others to follow you. The role of leadership is to articulate expectations for growth toward excellence . . . clearly.

When leaders work from a clear, comprehensive master plan that features a core that is valued by and visible to all, they then have a solid platform from which to communicate their vision.

In the end, your clarity is essential to the understanding of those whose understanding is essential to your success.

This book embraces the core assumption that clarity of purpose is an essential quality of effective leadership. If you want people to follow you, you must lead with a clarity of purpose that is evident in your own words and deeds.

VI. Embody the Change

Mahatma Gandhi taught us, first by example and later with words, to ". . . *be* the change you want to see in the world."

It is worthwhile, of course, to speak well of the changes we wish to create. It is also worthwhile to safeguard our actions to assure that we do not act in conflict with the changes we wish to create. But . . .

Until we embody the changes we wish to create, our leadership is incomplete.

As stated in the earlier section on "clarity of purpose," the clarity of one's own actions is vital. To say one thing and do another gives a damaging mixed message; even those who do not judge it harshly will surely be disheartened by it. If the new vision for change is one that requires staff to adopt a new mindset, then *everyone* must adopt that new mindset and *demonstrate* the new mindset impeccably. This, again, requires an act of deliberate focus.

For leaders, embodying the change means remaining visible and engaged no matter who else is leading any aspect of the project.

To accomplish organization-wide change, some delegation of duties is essential. But when implementing substantive organizational changes, handing off day-to-day leadership duties to another visible leader creates a situation we must manage carefully. If a leader at the executive level chooses a project leader to manage the change, he or she then has the choice of either fading out of the spotlight or remaining visible. It is essential that leaders of change remain visible in support of the desired change no matter what leadership tasks they delegate.

This book embraces the core assumption that we can do whatever it takes to bring the change about when we are willing to be the change we want to see.

VII. Pay Attention to What You *Want*

If we pay attention to our problems we'll get more problems; if we pay attention to our successes we'll get more success.

One of our favorite truisms at CHCM is "You get what you pay attention to." This concept (a first cousin to Appreciative Inquiry) shines light not only on the power of our attention, but on our ability to place our attention (to *focus*) wherever we wish to. This may seem obvious to some, but it's something to which most of us give too little thought. We may know that we *can* place our attention wherever we wish, but how often do we practice consciously placing our attention where it would do us the most good? For example, many of us will automatically give our attention to things that make us feel terrible just because they are "important." When there is a tragedy unfolding before our eyes (even if it's only unfolding on television) it doesn't occur to many of us that it is possible for our attention to be anywhere but squarely on the details of the tragedy.

In leading organization-wide change, it's important to remember that it is entirely your responsibility to deliberately place your attention on that which you wish to increase—things like your organization's known strengths, its actions and behaviors that have been successful in the past and your vision for the future.

If you are one who will lead organization-wide change, you are bound to meet some resistance from a few vocal naysayers in your organization. In any major change you'll have a small percentage of people who embrace the change enthusiastically; a small percentage of people who want no part of the change; and a large percentage in the middle who will adopt a "wait and see" stance. In Mary Koloroutis's *Transformational Leadership Cycle* (2004), one of the elements of the model challenges us to "go with the energy." This means putting the vast majority of our attention on that group of enthusiastic embracers of change and harnessing their energy to pull the effort forward. This is one of those great ideas that takes, for most of us, a major change of habit.

In CHCM's *Leading an Empowered Organization* workshop, we use something called the "2-8 Rule" to help us bring as many individuals as possible into alignment with the organization's vision for change.

The 2-8 Rule refers to the notion that in any given group there's a bell-curve distribution of folks who are naturally positive (12-15% on the right end of the curve) and who upon hearing of something new will readily support it, assuming it resonates with their values. At the other end there is an equal number of folks who can be counted upon *not* to support it initially. In the middle are the majority who will wait and see how elements of the change play out.

Wise leaders focus on what's positive so they'll get more of it. And, wise leaders also articulate the expectation that *all* will move toward the stated goal, and that we have choices as to how and when—but not as to *whether*—we will all move toward the goal.

Those on that left end—those who can be counted on *not* to immediately support the change— and some in the middle may need to have anywhere from 2 to 8 meaningful conversations about the proposed change—its implications, its benefits and so on—before they'll sign on.

The 2-8 rule alerts us to the need to forgive past behavior that appears to be negative or resistant. It guides leadership to incorporate into its plan for change 2-8 opportunities for people to learn enough about the change to make them willing (and sometimes even eager) to participate in it.

As for those who still choose not to participate, leaders will regretfully honor their choice and will express regret that they will be missed. Absenting one's self from the process of change while still employed is not an option.

Know that it is possible for you to listen to a list of everything that's "wrong" with your plan and still place your attention squarely on your tried and true methods, your airtight plans and the enthusiastic few.

Imagine the response if managers were to routinely ask staff, "What is the most professionally exciting situation you're involved in today?" Now consider the response if managers routinely asked staff, "How are you surviving?" What we pay attention to shapes our experience both broadly and deeply. Eventually caregivers working with the manager who enquired about their survival would come to believe they were lucky to make it to the end of their shifts in one piece. And eventually—fortunately—caregivers working with the manager who asked about professionally exciting situations would come to believe they worked on a unit that was professionally exciting. It's a powerful change of focus worth practicing.

> *This book embraces the truism that "you get what you pay attention to" because we've seen the careful, deliberate placement of our attention make projects immensely successful.*

VIII. Put Patients and Families First

> *Our patients and their families rest at the very heart of effective, fulfilling professional practice.*

This is always easy to say, and it is sometimes even easy to practice. But designing an organization's infrastructure so that its every role, practice, system and process advances what's best for patients and their families is another matter entirely. Because organizational action planning doesn't happen at the point of care, it is only when we keep our patients and their families in the full light of our consciousness—*while constructing our plans for change*—that we can design infrastructures that truly put patients and families first.

It seems almost impossible that we would have systems in place that do not already actively advance the best care for our patients, but it is essential that we look closely at all of our systems to see the degree to which they truly support patient-driven professional practice.

> *If a system is 80% in support of professional practice, we celebrate that 80% success and then refine that system to make it actively advance professional practice—100%.*

Throughout any period of change, the details can be so numerous that it's easy to get lost in them. We in health care, however, always have a beacon to guide us. If we experience even one moment of confusion about why we do what we do, we have only to remember our commitment to our patients and their families to figure out our next step. We need only to ask ourselves, "What can I do *now* to help create the best experience possible for our patients and their families?"

This book embraces the core assumption that those who have chosen to provide care to people at their most vulnerable do so because they want to care compassionately and competently and they want to make a difference in the lives of the patients and families they serve.

The Guiding Principles of Change

- Make Every Inquiry "Appreciative"
- We Have Influence
- Experience Exuberance
- Believe in Your Abundance
- Be Clear
- Embody the Change
- We Get What We Pay Attention To
- Patients and Families Come First

PART

II

Fundamentals of I_2E_2

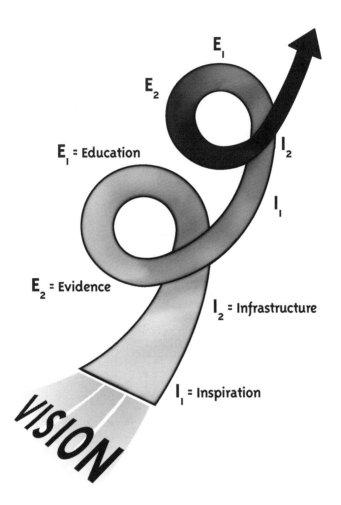

E₁

E₂

E₁ = Education

I₂

I₁

E₂ = Evidence

I₂ = Infrastructure

I₁ = Inspiration

VISION

2

The Benefits of I_2E_2

Imagine a hospital with a vision statement that reads something like "To be the health care provider and employer of choice for our communities."

To accomplish its broad and admirable goal, the organization measures performance outcomes in various aspects of its functioning. When it finds success, it celebrates that success, and when it finds a lack, it addresses the lack. Over time, the organization finds itself sponsoring a number of task forces simultaneously to address each of its concerns individually, in hopes of giving each comprehensive attention. Each task force has been set up in order to either directly improve the care experience of patients and their families or fix an identified "problem." This hospital sponsors task forces on:

1. patient safety

2. nurse recruitment and retention

3. patient processing

4. documentation

5. nurse-physician relationships

6. customer service

7. JCAHO Survey/Magnet Designation™/ Baldrige Award

8. disaster responsiveness

9. HIPAA implementation

10. myriad other initiatives related to any problems or new priorities identified by hospital leaders

Each group is headed by a competent leader, and each group collects valuable information and has to its credit visible improvements in the organization. But in this hospital, each task force is often working independently and with little communication between the groups. Subsequently, a fair amount of duplication of efforts results. The task forces generate lots of good ideas but for all of their good work, they ultimately serve as distractions to improving the overall organization because they are not integrated by a well-defined core purpose.

This health care organization would benefit from giving all of these groups a single focus, or at least clarifying where their efforts "fit" into a larger vision.

If these task forces were all pointed toward a common *specific* vision, the individuals within them could begin to think of each other as colleagues, a new level of collegiality would emerge, and duplication of efforts would be reduced.

I_2E_2 helps leaders create action plans that tie existing work to a central core.

If, for example, this organization chose to become a Relationship-Based Care (RBC) organization, the work and goals of each task force would consistently center on achieving their organization-specific principles of RBC (i.e., the accountability and continuity of patient-caregiver relationships). Imagine how this new focus would reshape how the organization handled its nurse recruitment and retention. Imagine also how it would serve to refocus the efforts of those working on patient safety, patient processing, documentation and nurse-physician relationships. Imagine how an RBC focus would give a whole new meaning to the term "customer service."

We're talking about major organizational change here. It doesn't happen overnight, and it doesn't happen by mandate. It happens over months (and more often 3-5 years), and it happens by consensus. This is where I_2E_2 can help.

When an organization finds itself ready to commit to a whole new way of being, I_2E_2 provides a formula to ensure that all planning and implementation activities for that change are comprehensive and inclusive.

When organizations are ready to rein in all of their related task forces and tie them to a common purpose, I_2E_2 is a proven formula for designing, implementing and sustaining comprehensive integrated cultural change. And perhaps I_2E_2's greatest benefit is that it encourages *the engagement of everyone in the organization*, helping to maximize individual contributions on behalf of the collective good.

While this book will concern itself largely with the ways in which I_2E_2 can be used for planning, it is important to note that because I_2E_2 is cyclical in nature, it is also an effective formula for actively leading, managing and sustaining change. It becomes the blueprint, or "knitting pattern", to which project leaders can refer in order to gauge the status and progress of any aspect of the plan.

The Knitting Pattern

So often in health care we have seen plans for change fizzle because the reality is that "life happens" all day every day, and we respond to what happens as best we can. We may try to penetrate that reality with a new focus on some specific change we want to see in our organization, but the reality is still that we will invariably end up putting aspects of that change aside for periods of time—and then at some point (we hope not too much later) we'll pick them up again.

A few years ago, Rob Whieldon, a colleague in the United Kingdom, was coordinating the training of more than 1000 *Leading an Empowered Organization* facilitators. The work plan that kept him and everyone else on the right page and moving forward was an intricate timetable he called his "knitting pattern." This ingenious piece of coordination captured the complexity of managing the training process and made it simple to assess where they were in the process at any given time.

Very few projects, from a knitted scarf to deep organizational change, are worked on without break from start to finish. We start projects and then put them down for many reasons, planning to pick them up later, hoping to be able to figure out both where we left off and what to do next. As you coordinate organizational change, I_2E_2 can act as your "knitting pattern"—your detailed action plan.

An I_2E_2 action plan allows Project Leaders to more clearly observe (and by extension, to communicate) the status of the effort to create change in the organization.

Just as you could check your knitting pattern to determine how far along your scarf is, you can use your I_2E_2 action plan to determine how far along your organization-wide change initiative is. I_2E_2 makes it easy for those leading change to reclaim their focus and stay inspired to bring a new vision to life.

From the novice to the seasoned pro, we've all played a part in creating changes that have worked. We've all played a part in creating changes that haven't worked. And we've all played a part in creating changes that worked for a while and then fizzled.

I_2E_2 will help you sustain *the changes you bring to your organization for as long as you want to sustain them.*

Once you complete a cycle of addressing each element of your original action plan, the cycle starts again as you readdress each element from the perspective of your newly changed (and continually changing) organization.

I_2E_2 doesn't deal in quick fixes, fragmented plans or "flavor-of-the-month" program implementations. It is useful for those with the patience to stick with a good plan long enough to achieve the payoff. The truth is we are all hungry for a way to bring together all the fragmented efforts in our organizations. I_2E_2 helps us do just that.

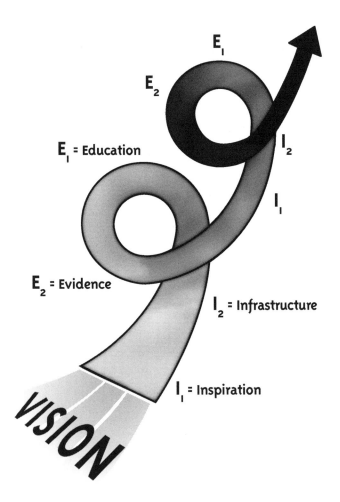

E_1

E_2

E_1 = Education

E_2 = Evidence

I_2

I_1

I_2 = Infrastructure

I_1 = Inspiration

VISION

3

Linking the Vision to Elements of I_2E_2

This chapter provides a comprehensive look at what goes into each of the four elements—Inspiration (I_1), Infrastructure (I_2), Education (E_1), and Evidence (E_2)—of the I_2E_2 action plan, and how those elements help us achieve our vision.

This section will help leaders of change devise action plans that "cover all the bases," leave nothing to chance and encourage the engagement of all individuals at every level of their organizations.

But what exactly is it we're setting out to create? To what, precisely, are we changing? A clear vision must be the first step in the change process.

Vision First

While I_2E_2 is indispensable in bringing visions to life, it is not in itself a vision, nor does it help you construct one. Your organization's vision must already be established before I$_2$E$_2$ can be of use to you. Strategic organizational vision statements like the one in the example in the previous chapter—"to be the health care provider and employer of choice for our communities"—may serve well as general statements of purpose, but they are neither specific nor comprehensive enough to function as statements of vision for real change in behaviors and systems.

Your organization's vision for change must be tangible enough for everyone in the organization to actually visualize it. It must contain details that bring it to life. It must provide a picture of what practice will really be like once the change is complete. And it must include elements that can be measured in order to verify at some point whether we have in fact achieved the realization of the vision.

Construct your vision with its end use in mind: It is to be used as a touchstone for all that you do on the way to making that vision *live* in the daily workings of your organization.

Visions must be accompanied by guiding principles and related behavioral and process outcome measures.

An example of an effective vision for change in a health care organization including target objectives follows:

In our organization:

- Patient satisfaction and staff satisfaction scores are above 90% by the end of the first year of implementation of Relationship-Based Care.

- Each patient's care is managed by one RN who establishes a therapeutic relationship at (or soon after) admission, and this relationship lasts throughout the patient's stay on the care unit.

- The patient and family are actively engaged in the development of a care plan driven by their expressed wishes.

- Physicians and nurses are partners in the patient care planning process. Care is attentive to the mind, body and spirit.

- Patients have the resources they need in a timely manner.

- The patient and family are satisfied because they believe that their number one expressed concern regarding this episode of care is also the number one priority for their RN and the health care team.

- The patient experiences caring as he or she describes caring upon admission.

Notice that I_2E_2 vision statements are written in the present tense. When we facilitate the development of vision statements in organizations, we ask that individuals express the details of their desired future as if they are already alive and thriving within the organization. This helps generate a clear, tangible direction, as it inspires people to get specific about how they will bring about the changes they desire.

Once the vision is articulated and clear behavioral outcomes are described, I_2E_2 becomes our formula for creating an action plan to bring that vision to life. The first element is Inspiration (I_1).

Inspiration (I_1):

Inspiration helps others to see that the benefits of change outweigh the risks of upsetting the status quo.

Inspiration ignites our passion—it creates energy in us. At its best, it helps us to see that it is our unique talents that make us valuable contributors to change. As these unique talents are present throughout the organization at every level, *everyone* has the potential to be inspired.

The best Inspiration is that which links the "new" collaborative vision to something that already exists in the people we wish to lead.

We inspire most effectively when we find within the people we intend to lead, the seeds of the new vision itself. Rather than thinking of the team we wish to inspire as a clean wall over which we will apply a new shade of paint, we will instead help them to see that the "new" vision is not so new—it's likely a vision they've held, and perhaps forgotten in the flurry of activity that has come to define their daily experience. If inspiration is to be lasting, it must be deep. It must bring the "new" collaborative vision into alignment with something that already exists in the people we wish to lead. This means communicating the vision for change core to core and heart to heart.

We chose health care as our field because we care about people and we want to help them through the times in their lives when they are their most vulnerable. Health care workers have a built-in core of caring, and it is this core that we can connect with when leading change. This implies that we can most effectively (or perhaps *only*) lead change when we as leaders embody that same core of caring.

Not surprisingly, inspiration and appreciation go hand in hand. It is through our expressions of appreciation that we let people know, perhaps more effectively than in any other way, that we truly *see* their contributions. When we recognize excellence in each other we inspire each other toward greater excellence. In an environment where appreciation flows freely, people believe that they have something valuable to contribute.

We get inspiration from our countless opportunities to experience truth, beauty, goodness and unity in our work.

Philosophy professor and author Tom Morris writes about inspiration in his book *If Aristotle Ran General Motors: The New Soul of Business* (Owl Books, 1998). He writes that in order for people to be inspired to excellence, they must have a sense that their work contains elements of truth, beauty, goodness and unity—what he calls "the four foundations of business and personal excellence."

Dr. Morris writes that there are four sides to our nature that must be respected and nurtured in order for us to feel happy in our work. Our intellectual side needs to feel that it is dealing in *truth*, which in the workplace shows up as accurate information, above-board dealings, and consistent, integral leadership.

The quality of *beauty* comes into play when we use our creativity to solve problems, when we work with an easy flowing efficiency and when our actions inspire joy and healing in others. Our moral side requires *goodness*; we feel balanced in the presence of it and unbalanced without it. If we are confident of our own goodness, we are more willing to take the kind of risks necessary to do truly extraordinary work. And finally there is the spiritual quality of *unity*. When people feel connected to each other, connected to their environment and connected to a noble cause, they can be inspired to do their best under even the most difficult circumstances. Morris asserts that "if the inner spirit of people is healthy, then the overall corporate spirit of the organization grows strong."

Dr. Morris's work sheds light on the very nature of inspiration. We have countless opportunities to experience truth, beauty, goodness and unity in our work, and we can take no end of inspiration from them whenever we recognize them.

In I_2E_2, we inspire each other by pointing to the potential for all of us to experience truth, beauty, goodness and unity in the changes we bring. As a leader constructing the Inspiration (I_1) section of your I_2E_2 action plan, ask yourself

- How will this change enhance the integrity of our organization?

- How will this change improve the experience of patients and families and colleagues?

- How will this change make each individual's practice more effective?

- How have we previously been successful in galvanizing others to overcome their resistance and to engage in positive change?

- What good things are already happening in the organization that we can connect to this new vision?

- How will we share the global vision with the organization as a whole?

- What inspires *me* most about this new vision for change?

The answers to all of these questions (and any number of questions like them) will help you target how best to inspire people in your unique organization. In this first stage of organizational change, we identify potential allies among those who appear to share our passions. These become the individuals to whom we give the greatest share of our attention in the earliest phase because it is they who become a large part of the energy that pulls the vision into being.

Infrastructure (I_2):

Design your organization's Infrastructure so that its every role, practice, standard, system and process actively advances the realization of your vision for change.

In order to successfully bring about the changes we want it is essential to integrate the concepts and principles of our new vision into existing practices, systems and processes. When creating an action plan for change there are three levels of infrastructure to consider: strategic, operational and tactical.

Strategic: Every organization has a strategic plan along with its mission, vision and values statements. It is crucial that the new vision becomes integrated into the existing statements and plans. The action plan to achieve RBC then becomes the means and the method for the expression of the mission, vision and values statements and the achievement of strategic plan objectives.

Strategic thinking is big-picture thinking—it's about overall direction and it includes broad areas of functional activity to achieve the end goals.

Strategic thinkers decide how best to create a sense of unity, not just in the organization itself, but in the health care community as a whole. Planning at the strategic level can help us bring our practices in line with nationwide norms and standards (or at least to use those norms and standards as points of departure).

The strategic aspect of infrastructure planning is also where we talk about the culture of the organization. Strategic plans set integrated cultural changes into motion—setting organizations to evolve into Learning Organizations (Senge, Kleiner, Roberts, and Ross, 1994), to integrate the principles of Servant Leadership (Greenleaf & Spears, 2002) or to design and implement their own unique versions of Relationship-Based Care. Such strategic initiatives begin as organization-wide initiatives and quickly shape how things happen at the patient services level as well.

In strategic action planning we address questions like:

- What can be done to support our core business?
- How could integrating the newest innovations in health care positively affect our organization?
- How could strengthening the visibility of organizational leaders promote a greater consensus for our vision for change?

- In what ways can the executive team and board advance the new vision for change?

- In what ways does RBC support our defined mission, vision and values?

Strategic leadership produces philosophical directives that in turn shape action planning at the operational and tactical levels.

Strategic action planning yields strategic imperatives with appropriate organizational goals and objectives. These strategic imperatives are so fundamental to the functioning of the organization that they ultimately affect who wants to work in the organization and who doesn't. Learning Organizations, Servant Leadership and RBC models are all examples of whole new cultural ways of *being*. If they are going to become *real* in any organization—if they are to provide over-arching direction and really live as the principles that guide us—they require direction set at the executive and board levels.

Our imperative is to consciously link what we're doing in our day-to-day practice to the mission, vision and values statements of the organization and to revise these statements if they are not in alignment with our current intentions. At the strategic level we make sure that our mission, vision and values statements live in the organization—and not just on a plaque on the wall.

Operational: The operational aspect of infra-structure deals with roles, standards, policies, organizational reporting structures, human resources, and financial, communication and work systems.

The operational level is where the vision comes to life in departments and units throughout the organization.

Operational considerations help us clarify departmental roles, relationships, systems, schedules and assignments. Here we ask how our policies, procedures, organizational charts and systems can bring the strategic plan to life in the organization.

This is also where any oversight teams, steering committees and results councils are formed. Accountability is a vital component in any organization's culture, and the formation of these guiding bodies helps everyone involved in the change to understand who is ultimately accountable for the changes being made. These bodies also provide individuals from every level of the organization with a clearinghouse to which they can bring their own innovative recommendations for realizing the organization's vision for change.

In operational action planning we ask ourselves:

- What practices already in place at the unit level actively advance the vision for change?

- What new systems or processes could support this new initiative?
- How can reporting structures be adjusted to advance the vision for change?
- How will this change affect job descriptions, performance appraisals, learning profiles, policies, standards, etc.?
- Whose support will we want to enlist when making department, team and unit-level changes?
- Who at the department level can be tapped for leadership?

Tactical: The tactical aspect of infrastructure deals with daily practices, routines and standards.

> ***The tactical level is where the vision comes to life at the individual level—at the point of care.***

No matter what other structures are in place, what happens at the individual level is where the "rubber meets the road." Even if the strategic vision clearly identifies all that we aspire to, if individual, day-to-day practices are not in place you still don't "have it." In short—if it doesn't live in practice and it isn't prominent in the shift report, it doesn't exist.

> ***Our circle of influence is greatest at the tactical level.***

While it is true that every aspect of infrastructure can be designed to advance the best possible patient/family experience, the tactical level is the level where the vision is experienced by patients, families and colleagues. Therefore the tactical level is one in which our circle of influence is as deep as it is wide. The tone that is set at the strategic level and the mechanisms put into place at the operational level come to life in the hands-on practices at the point of care.

In our planning at the tactical level, we ask ourselves:

- How can we assist individuals to translate the strategic vision into reality in their unique relationships with patients, families and colleagues?

- What will it take to support each caregiver and service supporter in their quest for the best? . . . one day at a time, one relationship at a time?

- What commitments can be made to support healthy work relationships?

A good Infrastructure reduces fragmentation and distracting efforts by unifying practices, standards, systems, processes and work groups throughout the organization.

Attention to changing operational infrastructure is essential if we wish to expand our impact beyond the efforts of individuals. Because infrastructure has so many facets, it brings people from all over the organization together to focus on a central vision for change. Because of I_2E_2's inclusion of infrastructure, it helps us to build a "place at the table" for every shareholder group at all levels of the organization.

The process of collaboratively redesigning your infrastructure to actively advance your vision for change creates opportunities for each department to express its unique translation of your vision's principles. It is vital that all innovations and expressions of the adopted principles related to the vision become embedded in the infrastructure of your organization. Close attention to this achievement will provide the greatest return on your overall investment.

Education (E₁):

In order to effectively bring individuals into the change, it is vital to provide for any learning initiatives necessary to ensure their early success.

Organizational change usually means that all or most of the individuals in the organization will be asked to do at least some things differently. In order to design the Education (E_1) element of the I_2E_2 formula, we assess the current knowledge and skills of our talent pool and determine what additional knowledge and skill-building will be necessary to advance the vision for change. There will be educational concerns for the leaders of change just as certainly as there will be for individuals elsewhere in the organization.

The implementation of a new vision for change often finds individuals prepared for the clinical or technical aspects of their roles, but perhaps not as adequately equipped in the interpersonal relationship or critical and creative thinking aspects. Thus, their overall capacity to perform as leaders in their roles is compromised.

These related skills are necessary for all individuals who will be expected to lead or even influence change. Leaders of change may educate themselves through independent research and study, through leadership workshops, or through other workshops and trainings pertaining more directly to the kinds of change they're hoping to advance in their organizations. These leaders may also seek the advice of others who have led changes similar to those they want to institute, or they may seek the guidance of consultants specializing in creating the kind of change necessary to make their vision come to life.

While it is very satisfying to develop an educational program under which everyone in the organization becomes competent in the requisite clinical and technical skills, it is imperative that our educational offerings not stop there. The new culture you're creating will likely necessitate changes in how interpersonal relationships are structured as well as how each individual's creative and critical thinking skills are challenged. In the end, our goal is to expand the capacities of those engaged in the change process, and most importantly, of those engaged in the delivery of care.

When designing plans related to your educational offerings, consider all of these domains—clinical/ technical, interpersonal relationships, critical and creative thinking, and leadership.

As this graphic illustrates, all three dimensions of competency must be met in order for individuals to emerge as leaders. This leadership can emerge at any level of the organization, and its power to advance a vision for change should not be underestimated.

When you offer a truly comprehensive staff development program to your workforce, employees feel they are competent not only to "do their jobs," but to manage their own relationships, do their own critical and creative thinking and make their own decisions on the job. This level of competency is one at which individuals can discover their own "voice" within the organization.

While offerings this comprehensive can represent a fairly large investment of time, energy and money, they offer an excellent return on investment in terms of staff satisfaction and decreased turnover.

The goal of your educational element, however, is not just to prepare individuals to do their newly refined jobs; it's also to help them feel prepared to engage in change in the first place. As the following graphic indicates, the development of competency is one of the steps enabling individuals to engage in change.

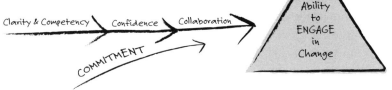

While this model has five components to it, its educational elements—clarity, competence and collaboration—create the momentum necessary for the rest of the model to fall into place with relative ease. When individuals see the organization's vision clearly, when they are clear about their roles and when individual practice supports these roles, individuals become ready to develop competencies to assure their success. When clarity exists and competency is achieved, staff feel prepared to carry out their part of the mission, and many emerge as leaders within their peer groups. They develop the confidence necessary to be effective collaborators, partnering with others on behalf of the patient and family. And when clearly focused, competent, confident individuals collaborate, their individual and collective commitment propels them forward as active agents of change.

Our Education (E_1) element comes together in response to questions like:

- What changes are we considering that would require additional learning for staff and managers at each level of our organization?

- What changes are we considering that would require additional learning for executives, medical staff or board members?

- What workshops would help provide a sense of the less tangible implications of the vision for change?

- How will newly employed staff be introduced to our expectations regarding this new vision and its implications on their roles?

- How might we help employees better manage their own relationships during and after the change?

- What new critical and creative thinking challenges will employees face during and after the change?

Education paves the way for excellence.

When individuals receive relevant, compelling learning experiences in clinical, interpersonal, critical and creating thinking and leadership skills, they become active participants in bringing the vision to life.

Evidence (E_2)

The Evidence element of I_2E_2 assesses how successful our efforts in Inspiration (I_1), Infrastructure (I_2) and Educational (E_1) are in advancing the organization's new vision.

Evidence is not to be regarded as judge and jury, however. It exists not to "critique" the changes, but to inspire greater commitment to the changes that have proven successful and to help redouble commitment to redesigning what has not yet proven successful. The assessment of evidence is one of the most obvious opportunities we have to practice Appreciative Inquiry. In I_2E_2 we recognize and celebrate any and all forward movement . . . remembering that creating a cultural change requires at least 3-5 years of focused effort.

Evidence makes visible the alignment of individual behaviors with the overall vision.

In a health care organization undergoing integrated cultural change, evidence helps us monitor the impact the new changes are making on our primary areas of concern—patient and family satisfaction and clinical quality. Furthermore, evidence helps us to monitor the impact of related variables like staff retention scores, nurse and physician satisfaction scores and other staffing-sensitive patient quality indicators—all of which ultimately affect patient loyalty, clinical quality and robust fiscal positioning.

The cyclical structure of I_2E_2 puts those who use it into position for continual review of progress.

At the end of each cycle we have a chance to appreciate our forward movement. We can discover what led to our successes, and we can ask ourselves what it would take to enhance or expand that success. This cyclical examination of evidence puts us on track to continually reinforce and strengthen successes while always reaching for new heights.

It is also both possible and advisable to measure "intangibles" like the degree to which employees are committed to—and work proactively for the advancement of—the organization's new vision. Not only are there measures that let us know whether we are committed, but there are even measures that let us know the extent to which we are a "we." Reflective practice and case reviews help us to measure these qualitative aspects, as do observational assessments of improvements in relationships between staff members and between staff and managers.

The Evidence (E$_2$) section of your action plan will respond to these questions:

- How will we determine that we have sustained our focus on the vision for change?

- What key process and outcomes measures—strategic, operational and tactical indicators—are most important to capture?

- What process of data collection and dissemination will be most inclusive and efficient?

- How will we ensure that all evidence collected becomes available for use as inspiration in future I$_2$E$_2$ cycles?

- How will we measure the commitment level of the staff?

- Who will manage the collection, analysis and dissemination of the new data measuring the effectiveness of this new initiative?

- How will we know when our vision for change is a reality?

As evidence is primarily compiled through measurement and evaluation, we tend to think of a body of evidence as a report card—we did what we were asked to do, our effectiveness was measured, and we got "graded" on what we did. With I_2E_2, however, evidence functions not as a conclusion, but as a springboard into a repetition of the entire formula. Evidence (E_2) provides material for Inspiration (I_1), which takes us back to Infrastructure (I_2), which takes us back to Education (E_1), and so on. That means we never get our grades and go home. It means that change is a dynamic and everlasting process. It means that every step leads to another step. It means that we inspire everyone in the organization to commit *continually* to the organization's vision, that we revise and improve infrastructure as needed, that we provide timely relevant education to individuals at all levels of the organization and that we gather evidence and *use it* as the inspiration to start new cycles of I_2E_2 again and again.

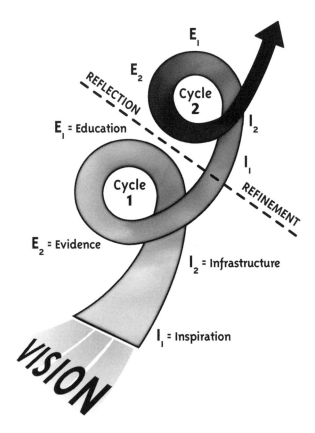

When all is said and done, leading sustainable change requires us to embrace the notion that change is constant.

4

Everyday Applications

In order to give you the clearest possible look at the ways in which the elements and principles of I_2E_2 are fundamental to successful, sustained change, I'd like to offer three quick scenarios—unrelated to health care—in which I_2E_2 provides a structure within which a plan for change is devised. Use these examples to experience how simple it is to let I_2E_2 work for you—and how the principles of I_2E_2 are working for you already, whether you realize it or not.

In the first scenario, notice how the elements of I_2E_2 apply to a plan for accomplishing an everyday task for which the majority of your "planning" is completely second nature.

Scenario One: Putting Fuel in Your Car

Vision: This week I have enough fuel in my vehicle to get to all of my destinations on time and without undue stress, as there will be no need for an extra stop for gas.

Inspiration (I_1): Having enough gas in my car helps me to arrive promptly at work and all of my appointments. I enjoy going to my local filling station because I like the people there and I like to support my community's small businesses.

Infrastructure (I_2): I will envision a successful trip to the gas station (strategic), consider which gas station to go to and when to go there as well as how I will pay for the gas (operational), and determine whether I will pump the gas myself or go to a full-service station (tactical).

Education (E_1): When I get to the station I will read the pump to select which octane gasoline I will put into my vehicle. I know from having once read the sticker on my gas cap that my car takes "premium" gas. I have built my gas-pumping skills over years of experience.

Evidence (E_2): I will see the evidence that I am filling my tank with fuel when I see the gauge change at the pump, and I will confirm that my tank is full when I read the gas gauge inside my car. I will know that I have succeeded in my overall endeavor if after one week I will not have had to make an additional stop for gas.

Clearly, I_2E_2 is not nearly as revolutionary as it is fundamental.

Nearly every task we undertake, no matter how small, contains elements of Inspiration (I_1), Infrastructure (I_2), Education (E_1) and Evidence (E_2) whether we are conscious of them or not. When we become conscious of them, however, we can use them deliberately to accomplish what we want to accomplish with less worry about any details we might have forgotten.

Here is another everyday example. This time we'll look at a project that requires a slightly higher level of deliberate planning.

Scenario Two: Painting a Bedroom

Vision: The walls of my bedroom are painted in a color that feels warm and restful to me. The new color brings out the green in the bedspread. Our entire family helps accomplish this vision; we work together efficiently and harmoniously.

Inspiration (I_1): I am inspired by my vision of a freshly painted bedroom. My spouse and I recently purchased a new bedspread, and we are enjoying the prospect of finding a paint color that brings out the green in it.

Infrastructure (I_2): My spouse and I will determine what sort of color would best accomplish our vision of the overall "look" we're seeking (strategic), determine our budgetary parameters and time limitations (operational), plan which paint store to go to and when to go there (operational), decide what method of payment to use to pay for the paint (operational), and determine whether we will paint the walls ourselves or ask our children to help us (operational); finally, we will determine work style preferences and schedules to suit each of the painters (tactical). I will also set timelines for the completion of the entire project (strategic) as well as for any interim steps (cleaning, taping around trim, moving furniture, etc.) leading up to the completion of the project (operational).

Education (E_1): The person working at the paint store will be able to answer all of my questions regarding the best sort of paint, brushes, rollers, drop cloths and paint pans to use for this project. My spouse and I have developed prior painting skills through various painting tasks we've taken on over the years. Since we've decided to ask our teenage children to help us, my spouse and I will teach them all of the techniques necessary to paint neatly and effectively without any mishaps—*before* we formally begin the project.

Evidence (E_2): I will measure our success by how much we like the color of our walls, whether the color we select brings out the green in the bedspread and what we perceive to be the overall feeling in the bedroom when the walls are painted. I'll measure our commitment to this project by whether we keep to the established timelines for interim steps, make no additional trips to the paint store for supplies and finish the entire project by the deadline we set. Success will also mean that painting the room was a satisfying family activity.

Admittedly, the prospect of sitting down with paper and pencil to devise a plan for painting a room may feel a little silly. But painting a room is just the kind of task many of us would normally undertake with too little thought. Once you get a feel for how I_2E_2 works, devising a plan like the one above might take you about 10 minutes. (Compare that to the time it takes to run back to the paint store for more supplies.)

In the next scenario, an individual commits to losing 20 pounds and improving his physical stamina. This example is fleshed out with even more details. And unlike the more bare-bones scenarios before it, this example concludes with information about how the I_2E_2 plan is designed to cycle indefinitely to help sustain the changes we create. First we'll look at the thought processes that go into devising each element of the plan and then a full action plan will follow a few pages later.

Notice how using I_2E_2 helps you reach into the dimly lit corners of your planning to ensure that you consider every element that will contribute to your success.

Scenario Three: Losing 20 Pounds and Improving Physical Stamina

Vision: I lose 20 pounds in 18 weeks and improve my physical stamina to where I can ride a bike for one hour with ease.

This time, before we launch into the actual I_2E_2 plan, let's look at the thinking behind each element.

Inspiration (I_1): It may seem initially that the inspiration in this scenario would come from the individual's dissatisfaction with his current physical condition. But inspiration does not come from assessing problems; it comes from envisioning solutions, considering past and current successes and believing that the desired vision is possible. In a project like this one, his inspiration may come from envisioning how pleasurable it will be to live in his desired state of physical well-being and by recalling his past successes with weight loss, weight maintenance and physical conditioning.

Infrastructure (I_2): He realizes immediately that strategic planning will be essential to his success. He'll set clear goals about what he wants to accomplish: loss of 20 pounds and the ability to ride a bike with ease for one hour. He determines that he will accomplish his goal within 18 weeks. Operationally, he'll contemplate the financial considerations of his new venture (clothing, shoes, class costs, health club membership, etc.) as well as where he will work out and whether he will get any personal training assistance or take any classes. He'll check his daily schedule to see how much time he can reasonably devote to his new fitness concern, and he'll decide whether he's willing to make any adjustments in his current schedule to make more room for activities related to this project. Tactically he'll consider what time of day he will work out and how his overall routine will change in order to make fitness a lasting priority.

Education (E$_1$): As he tends to the infrastructure concerns around his new fitness project, he may quickly realize that he has some research to do. He'll call health clubs in his area asking about prices, trial memberships, locations, specialty classes and personal training options. He'll think about what other forms of exercise (besides just biking) that he would enjoy doing. He'll also ask friends and associates for guidance on diet and nutrition books, peruse several and decide what looks like a promising dietary course for him.

Evidence (E$_2$): Since he has two specific goals (losing 20 pounds and gaining the ability to ride a bike with ease for one hour), he determines that he'll arrange to collect specific evidence for each goal. In order to create smaller cycles of success, he decides he'll set six 3-week periods in which to lose three and one-half pounds each, and increase his time on the bike by 7.5 minutes per period as he can currently ride with ease for 30 minutes. He will create a chart on which he will plot his progress both weekly and biweekly.

Continuing the Cycle: This man is expecting to set up his evidence element in a way that lends itself easily to six 3-week cycles of I_2E_2. After each of his six set periods, he could reassess his Inspiration (I_1), Infrastructure (I_2), Education (E_1) and Evidence (E_2) concerns and tweak them—or even redesign them if they prove unworkable in some way—for each subsequent cycle.

For any plan to create lasting change, the plan must continue in some form even once the desired goal is achieved.

In this case, the plan to lose 20 pounds has an end point. But maintaining our ideal weight and keeping physically fit are lifelong endeavors. Once the initial weight loss is complete, repeating the cycle of I_2E_2 monthly or quarterly—revisiting the Inspiration (I_1), Infrastructure (I_2), Education (E_1) and Evidence (E_2) elements pertinent to maintaining optimum health—will help him stay on course for as long as he chooses. As his endeavor is largely individual, his vision and action plan are too. (Even with plans for organization-wide change, personal vision and personal action are the backbone of organizational success.)

What follows is an I_2E_2 action plan in its final format for the implementation of a program to lose 20 pounds and gain the ability to ride a bike for one hour.

Vision: I lose 20 pounds in 18 weeks and improve my physical stamina to the point where I can ride a bike for one hour with ease.

Inspiration (I_1): I take time daily to envision myself the way I want to look and feel.

I remember that I once maintained my desired weight for a period of 3 years through portion control and biking regularly outside when weather permitted and indoors at home in inclement weather.

I journal daily, focusing on what I am enjoying most about this project.

Infrastructure (I_2): I budget $300 as an initial investment for new athletic shoes, clothing, three personal training sessions and the repair of the rear tire on my bike.

I keep to a budget of $125/ month for gym membership and various ongoing expenses related to fitness.

I choose the YMCA as my gym because it is conveniently located and it offers the classes and training I want.

I take a spinning class on Monday nights at my gym.

I work with a personal trainer for three sessions over 6 weeks to make sure I'm on the right track.

I work out Monday and Wednesday evenings and Saturday afternoons, doing either weight training and a bike ride at my gym or a bike ride outdoors.

I faithfully reschedule any workouts I miss due to other commitments.

I create and use a daily log to keep track of my food and water intake and the consistency of my participation in my exercise program.

I ask my wife to talk with me each week about my progress.

Education (E$_1$): I call the club to inquire about personal trainers and interview at least two trainers over the phone to determine who might be a good match for me.

I review portions of the *Diet X* book to determine whether I'd like to use it as my dietary guide.

I skim the *Diet Y* book to see whether it has anything I'd like to incorporate into my plan to eat better.

I check out a weight loss program and will decide after 2 weeks on my program if joining would help me meet my goals.

Evidence (E$_2$): By the end of week two of my program, I have determined exactly what dietary program to follow.

By the end of week three I have completely transitioned to my new dietary program.

By the end of week three I have lost 3.5 pounds.

By the end of week three I have increased my time on the bike by 3-4 minutes.

By the end of each 3-week period I have worked out at least nine times.

I review my daily log on a weekly basis to assess my commitment to this project.

Commitment to Future Cycles of I_2E_2: Every 2 weeks, I rework my I_2E_2 action plan to reflect what I know at that point that I didn't know before.

Incorporating a plan to sustain change is essential to the long-term success of any endeavor.

In future cycles of I_2E_2 this man will incorporate what he learns from his personal trainer and alter his routine to reflect the trainer's recommendations. And as the first cycle of I_2E_2 has him still educating himself about diet (and as finding the ideal diet is somewhat a matter of trial and error), he may also make some dietary changes in later cycles. He may also find that his goal of increasing his time on the bike by only 3-4 minutes per 3-week cycle is too easy for him and after the first cycle of I_2E_2 he may increase that goal.

While you may never use I_2E_2 for this sort of personal planning, this scenario helps demonstrate how I_2E_2 helps you to be comprehensive and stay committed. This last example in particular points to how essential it is to plan for sustaining your change. All of us have either experienced or witnessed how easy it is for extra weight and sedentary behavior to creep back into people's lives even after a substantial period of successful fitness management. The same is true with organization-wide change. Once positive changes are successfully up and running, it's not discouragement that derails them. Far more often it is simply a lack of sustained focus on what we want.

> *I_2E_2, with its comprehensive, cyclical nature, ensures that we stay focused on sustaining the changes we've worked hard to create.*

I_2E_2 provides a methodology to help you create, implement and evaluate a plan for change. It helps you put a plan in place that allows you to know when you have achieved your desired future. It's a way to create a plan that helps you consider every element in the process of change so that no detail is overlooked and its cyclical structure helps you sustain the changes you desire for as long as you choose to sustain them.

PART

III

I_2E_2 Reflection:
The BIDMC Merger

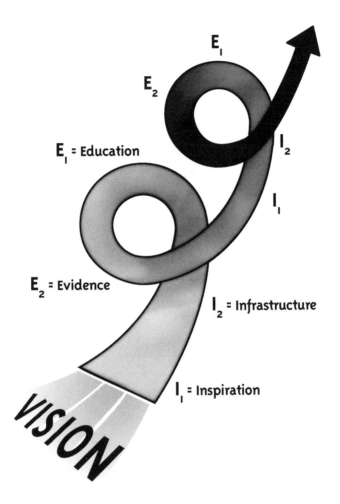

E_1

E_2

E_1 = Education

E_2 = Evidence

I_2

I_1

I_2 = Infrastructure

I_1 = Inspiration

VISION

5

What Happened?

Many in health care are familiar with the story of the troubled merger of Boston's Beth Israel and New England Deaconess hospitals that began in the late 1990s. In a book called *Code Green: Money-Driven Hospitals and the Dismantling of Nursing*, Dana Beth Weinberg tells the story of two hospitals with vastly different cultures merging as a way to stay competitive in the era of managed care. While the author points to the notion that money concerns were "driving the boat" for the duration of the change, it is apparent that something else—something vital— was missing for those working through the beginning stages of the merger.

Code Green *is, to my eyes, the story of two hospitals with two visions that could not become one hospital because they could not—or perhaps would not— agree on a shared vision for change.*

Beth Israel was a hospital known for its care-driven professional nursing practice. It followed a Primary Nursing model and was for decades a successful, highly esteemed hospital. New England Deaconess was known for its operational efficiency. It had become a model in the industry for streamlining and cutting costs without sacrificing clinical quality. Both hospitals operated "in the black" and both hospitals boasted dedicated workforces, proud of what they were able to accomplish within the cultures they had established.

And then they merged.

This chapter is not a postmortem on a failed merger. (First, that wouldn't be helpful to anyone, and second, the hospitals are now very successfully merged.) This chapter is yet another look at how the elements of I_2E_2 are essential to successful, sustained change—and more specifically here, how tragically and needlessly difficult change is without them.

A Shared Vision for Change

It is naïve, of course, to think that those leading mergers don't give broad consideration to the full scope of the changes they are leading. While *Code Green* seems to suggest that there was in fact a failure of leadership to carefully manage the nuances of the change, there seems to be a larger issue—the lack of a *clearly articulated* vision for change—that made this merger, in its initial stages, so troubled.

When Beth Israel and Deaconess began their merger into Beth Israel Deaconess Medical Center (BIDMC), the BIDMC executive team brought doctors and nurses together to show them a presentation that included details of the proposed merger. The presentation highlighted many changes, some of which had already been in the works prior to the merger, and the information was presented in such a way that it was the perception of many of those present that BIDMC executives were taking credit for masterminding changes that others had already suggested and had even been working on (the perception may or may not have been accurate, but the perception mattered a lot). Leaders may well have presented a vision for change, but to the eyes and ears of those they intended to lead into a new era, their presentation fell short of including, engaging or even acknowledging those already doing great work in the organization. They missed a golden opportunity to harness the early enthusiasm of those already working in the direction of the change by offering the impression that they did not value or even recognize their efforts.

A vision for change must be inclusive. It must be engaging. It must acknowledge the contributions of those already on board and the potential contributions of those we wish to bring on board.

Inspiration (I_1):

With no overtly stated inclusive, engaging vision to unify the focus of individuals at the two hospitals, efforts to inspire the workforce were often met with open scorn. Each organization had tremendous success to point to (as later leaders discovered and embraced), but without a unifying vision, aspects of care, like the nursing programs in particular, became competitive rather than cooperative. It is stated more than once in *Code Green* that nurses from each hospital took the position that if someone asked them to do something differently, that same someone was clearly saying they'd been doing it "wrong" all along. Without a vision that acknowledged the best of what everyone was already doing, the fundamental differences between the nursing models embraced by the two hospitals fueled a "we versus them" stance that took the organization years to stand down.

> *Inspiration must say, "This is what is beautiful about what you are doing now," before it can inspire anyone to do anything beyond what he or she is already doing.*

It was only in later stages of the merger that leaders embraced this method of inspiration. Early on, the refrain from the administration was "We can't go back to doing things the way we used to," which leaves speculation about what we *can* do not only wide open, but, by implication, off the conference table completely. It wasn't until a few years into the merger that staff embraced a new administrative team that it believed valued them enough to really listen to what they needed. This listening is a strong contributor to the element of Inspiration (I_1). Active listening followed by careful, respectful, reasoned response is always inspiring.

> **If you intend to inspire, you must be able to honestly say, "*I* see *your success because I really see what you're doing, and I* hear *your success because I'm really listening.*"**

Perhaps the greatest tragedy in the BIDMC merger's early days was leadership's apparent failure to recognize and leverage some of the really wonderful things that were going on in the two organizations. As Weinberg discovered in a 1999 focus group, nurses and surgeons at the old Beth Israel had made patient rounds together every morning, creating greater collegiality between doctors and nurses while helping everyone involved to be as well prepared for their shifts as possible. At the old Deaconess, nurses had established a teamwork system through which they supported each other in taking regular lunch breaks and always leaving on time thus ensuring better self-care for nurses. These were both strengths within each pre-merger organization. And while they may seem at first glance almost antithetical to each other, the prevailing mindset that "We can't go back to doing things the way we used to" shut down any kind of questioning that may have made it possible for versions of each to peacefully coexist in the same organization. Focusing on what's possible gets us a lot farther that focusing on how things "can't" be.

Inspiration happens when we open ourselves to possibilities and seek to bring others along with us into the best that is possible from the best of what is.

Infrastructure (I_2):

When Beth Israel and New England Deaconess merged they had very different systems and procedures. In one often-cited example, the color used to flag physicians' orders needing to be filled had differed in the two hospitals before they merged. The merger happened before the "detail" of which color would be used to flag unfilled orders was decided. As a result, if a doctor from one campus was working at the other, the doctor often found that his or her orders were ignored. According to Weinberg, the eventual decision of which color to use to flag the orders took two years to make.

By the account given in *Code Green*, there was such a lack of unity (demonstrated most often as competitiveness) in the administrations of the two hospitals—even after they were, in name at least, *one* hospital—that decisions of nearly every kind took too long to even matter. If, for example, two extremely different groups of nurses were to merge their practices *before* a vision was established for what the new nursing program would look like, and *before* it was established which aspects of practice already in place at the two hospitals were working well, and *before* systems, processes and procedures were in place to support nurses in their work, the administration's eventual decisions on such matters could only be too little too late.

A good Infrastructure (I_2) always advances a unifying vision for change; it doesn't just help us to work well, it helps us to work well together.

The big Infrastructure (I_2) lesson from the BID-MC story is that a solid infrastructure that actively advances a shared vision must be in place *before anyone is asked to change his or her practice*. This issue is also related to the principle that clarity of purpose is essential to leading effective change. If we are to ask individuals to alter their practice and they ask, "How do I do that?" it is essential that we have something solid to point to in response. The Infrastructure (I_2) element of an I_2E_2 action plan ensures that the answer to that question is comfortingly concrete. Part of the answer to that question must always convey, "Here are the processes and systems now in place to make it possible for you to do what we're asking you to do."

In any period of change, input from those actually carrying out the work within the newly refined systems is also essential. Everyone must know where to take their innovative recommendations, even if it is to a clearinghouse or steering committee. This reassures individuals that they are playing an integral part in designing their own futures.

A well-constructed Infrastructure (I_2)—established prior to the changes we propose—provides a sense of relief to everyone involved in the change.

Education (E_1):

The story of the BIDMC merger also provides an informative backdrop against which to look at the role of Education (E_1) in organizational change. For example, prior to the merger, Beth Israel (where Primary Nursing was practiced) had the highest percentage of nurses in the country—94%—having four-year degrees. Many were even on their way to earning their Master of Science degrees. In contrast, the nursing staff at New England Deaconess, who worked within a model that had extensively utilized patient care technicians to do many of the "mundane tasks of nursing," had a much smaller percentage of nurses—43%—having four-year degrees. Much to its credit, the premerger Deaconess had provided an intensive three-month training program for its patient care technicians. But in an effort to cut costs, while BIDMC kept the patient care technician program intact, it switched to a training course only six weeks long for its technicians.

While it is not always inappropriate for educational initiatives to be abbreviated or even eliminated, it is essential that their worth be assessed with the overall vision of what is intended in the organization well fixed in mind. Again, this action seemed to bespeak a lack of clear vision for what the nursing program at BIDMC might ultimately look like. One camp was still fighting for Primary Nursing while another camp was hiring and training more patient care technicians, and *no* camp was establishing a clear vision of what nursing would look like at BIDMC.

The difference in the education levels of the nurses from the two hospitals made for other issues as well. Each premerger hospital had acquired the staff that made the most sense for the nursing model it embraced. When the two bodies merged, it was very hard for the Deaconess nurses not to see themselves as the "ugly stepsisters" in this story. Education is the great equalizer. While much was done to give Deaconess nurses as much rank and compensation as their Beth Israel counterparts, little was done in the early days of the merger to offer the educational opportunities that would have made them feel like their work was truly of equal value.

It is also important for leaders at the unit level to be adequately prepared to facilitate the transformation of their organizations. Again, in the case of BIDMC, the lack of vision for a unified, cohesive, well-defined nursing program had leaders positioned to compete rather than collaborate. And while it is essential for leaders at the unit level to develop excellent relationship and critical and creative thinking skills, even those, in the face of transformation without a clear vision for change, would have taken unit-level leaders at BIDMC only so far.

In I$_2$E$_2$, a good Education (E$_1$) element is always designed to directly advance the shared vision for change.

If we know what our patient care systems are supposed to look like and we have a clear sense of what our caregivers already know, we can figure out what is necessary for them to learn in order to bring the shared vision to life.

Evidence (E_2):

> *If we have a clear vision of who we want to be, we can figure out fairly simply how to determine when we've met that goal.*

To determine what to measure, we have only to assess the elements of our new proposed identity and to decide what new circumstances would provide evidence that we are embodying that new identity. If we do not have a concrete sense of who we want to be, it is impossible to know whether or not we've achieved our goal. The lack of a clearly articulated shared vision for change in the early stages of the BIDMC merger made it virtually impossible for the leaders of that change to know how to measure whether or not the hospitals were successfully merged.

The two premerger hospitals embraced Evidence (E_2) in almost as vastly different ways as they embraced nursing. While they measured many of the same indicators, and while they both collected hard, verifiable data, the old Beth Israel culture was one that valued the less easily measured "intangibles" of nursing more than the old Deaconess culture did. As a result, when the newly merged (and already economically stressed) BIDMC was deciding on what sort of nursing model to embrace, the Deaconess camp was not the least bit swayed to Primary Nursing by the "touchy feely," "unmeasurable" case they perceived members of the old Beth Israel camp to be making for it. Under their current economic conditions, few in the organization felt they were in a position to get behind any sort of practice for which they felt there was not hard data correlated to obvious monetary benefit.

But again, determining the ultimate success of a merger requires a clear vision of what a successful merger would ultimately look like. Those who collect data will never run out of data to collect. But unless they determine what data to collect based on the data's ability to help the organization understand the extent to which it has brought its vision to life, much of the work they do will be wasted.

Collecting Evidence that helps us to verify where we are in relation to where we want to be is essential to any organization's forward movement.

The Story Continues

The book *Code Green* ends in the darkest hours of the BIDMC merger. If one looked no further than the story it tells, one would assume that the BIDMC merger was—and is still—a dismal failure. But the BIDMC merger story does *not* end with the tale of this distressing book. In fact, just as the *Code Green* story ended, a new CEO, Paul Levy, and a new nurse executive and Vice President of Patient Care Services, Dianne Anderson, came into the organization.

In this new phase of the merger, BIDMC had leadership that understood the importance of appreciating "what is" and then identifying the most deeply held values of those they sought to lead and shaping them into a viable vision for change.

Paul Levy and Dianne Anderson have graciously agreed to let me use BIDMC's success story—the *complete* story of the BIDMC merger—to illustrate how the principles of effective change and all of the elements of I_2E_2 come into play in the leadership of any successful, sustainable change.

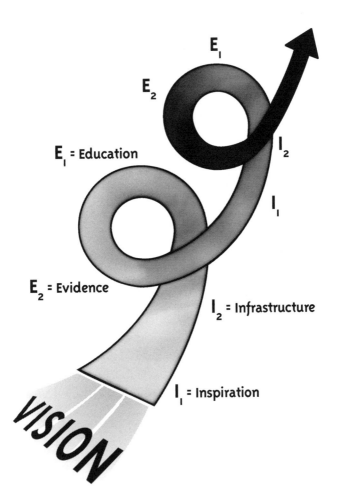

E_1

E_2

E_1 = Education

I_2

I_1

E_2 = Evidence

I_2 = Infrastructure

I_1 = Inspiration

VISION

6

All Elements in Place

In December of 2005, almost 10 years after the launch of the BIDMC merger, I had the opportunity to talk with Paul Levy and Dianne Anderson about the experience of coming into an organization that was, in Levy's words, "hemorrhaging money—losing 40-70 million dollars a year . . . with the loss rate the summer Dianne arrived of 8 or 9 million dollars a month," and perhaps even more dire, an organization in which "there was no hope. . . . The place was totally and utterly demoralized. . . . Many people had left over the course of the previous 5 years because they felt the place had gone sour and it wasn't going to succeed."

Levy and Anderson recognized early on that their greatest liability—the dire condition of both the organization's finances and its staff—was exactly where they would start.

They knew their first hurdle was to gain the trust of those who had been so sorely misused by previous administrations. They did this in four significant ways: 1) They made themselves physically visible throughout the hospital and *unmistakably accessible* to those whose trust they sought; 2) they initiated a culture of transparency, routinely asking for and sharing information with everyone in the organization; 3) they asked caregivers what they needed *most* in order to provide the kind of care they felt called to provide; and 4) they always did exactly what they said they would do.

A Shared Vision for Change

In our interview, Paul Levy bristled initially at the notion that he would have presumed to create a vision for the organization—one that he and his administrative team would determine themselves and impose on others. It became clear as we continued, however, that this did not mean that there was no vision for change; it meant only that the organization's vision emerged organically *from those working directly with patients* and took its shape little by little as the specific needs of those caregivers surfaced. Both Anderson and Levy came to BIDMC with the vision of not only making the organization financially solvent, but of "restoring the organization to its position as one of the world's great hospitals." How exactly that would happen was—initially, at least—something neither of them presumed to know.

> **The staff they found at BIDMC were extremely dedicated but not, as Levy is quick to point out, dedicated to BIDMC.**

The staff they found were dedicated to the *values* of BIDMC. To Anderson and Levy, this was significant. While prior leaders had put their attention on the countless ways in which Beth Israel and New England Deaconess had failed to successfully merge, Anderson and Levy had their attention on the fact that nearly everyone in the organization showed up for work every day for the same reason—to alleviate human suffering.

Levy and Anderson's vision for the organization found its foundation in this shared value. When I asked Levy whether when he arrived he saw BIDMC as one merged hospital or two organizations refusing to become one (and one could reasonably have chosen to see either), he said, "The values of the two hospitals have always been the same. These are hospitals; they are academic medical centers. They are set up to take really good care of people, to do very good research, and to do very good teaching. So the irony of the failure of the merger was that you had two organizations that basically believed in the same thing and had different ways of practicing it." Levy and Anderson harnessed the energy of this shared value and immediately sent the message (in actions as well as words), "We know what you care about, and by the way, we care about it too." The shared vision for change at BIDMC came from an understanding of the core values present throughout the organization: The whole staff was there to alleviate human suffering. Levy says modestly, "I think all we did was take the sense of values and the sense of mission that the people in the place already had, and we helped them to find a way to carry it out."

Even when Levy and Anderson sought advice from outside of the organization, they always put more stock in the wisdom and integrity of their own staff than in anyone else.

"We hired a consulting firm called the Hunter Group which made a number of suggestions," says Levy. "We put that report on our web site and asked people in the organization to review it, and when they disagreed with the Hunter Group's recommendations to give us suggestions for what else we might do. And then we pulled together our management group and in about a month wrote the turnaround plan, which was our blueprint for getting out of trouble. It involved layoffs; it involved efficiencies; it involved all kinds of things. And likewise we published that on the web site, and asked everybody to read it and to understand what their part was in it. Ultimately," Levy adds, "we eliminated 600 positions—or 10% of the workforce—only 300 of which were filled and none of whom were nurses."

Asking their staff what they needed in order to practice quality medicine and professional nursing was Levy and Anderson's way of leading the staff into envisioning things the way they wanted them to be. Few, if any, in the organization were in a position to visualize a "Utopian" care system; it would have been too big a jump. Instead they began with small steps, asking staff what barriers to quality care they wanted removed first. Levy states, "Almost everything they asked for was [to change] something that was getting in the way of their providing the kind of care to patients that they believed in."

The complete list of the well-thought-out requests of frontline caregivers essentially became the organization's shared vision for change.

Inspiration (I_1):

The first really inspiring thing Levy and Anderson did was to be open with everyone about the present condition of the organization, about how they hoped to turn it around and about the fact that *everyone's opinion would be heard* regarding how best to achieve solvency. This immediately felt different to the staff at BIDMC, and coupled with the visibility of the new senior management team, it went a long way toward winning the trust of those of whom big things would be asked.

"We spent a lot of time walking around the place and being accessible to people and hearing their comments and their suggestions, not only in the town hall meetings, but on the floors and in the corridors," says Levy. "I think that was important, but I don't feel like we were trying to convince people that they should have hope. What we were doing was being extremely respectful and trusting of the people who worked here. We knew they were all well intentioned and experts at what they did."

> *"We knew that in essence, if we got out of their way—if we got the organization out of their way," says Levy, "that they could just do their jobs and they would feel good."*

Levy's words reveal another aspect of the culture they created—and one not to be made small: They infused the culture with kindness. They listened and responded respectfully to people. They recognized and appreciated staff at all levels for their good ideas and their willingness, after all they'd been through, to share them. One almost gets the picture of people peeking out of their doors for the first time after a violent storm. They sniff the air and look around to see whether it is safe and, if it is, they may venture out. When those who had been so embattled for so long at BIDMC ventured out, they were as relieved by what they saw of the new administration as they could have hoped to be.

> **They saw people who appreciated their values and respected both their intelligence and their abilities—and it had been quite a while since they'd had the sense that anyone really had.**

The next step in inspiring the staff—and one that necessarily followed quickly—was to rack up some early successes. "How do you build trust?" asks Levy rhetorically. "You say what you are going to do and then you do it." And at BIDMC, that's exactly what they did. And they did it without cash flow.

Not surprisingly, however, while always conscious of their dire cash flow issues, Levy and Anderson put the majority of their focus not on what they lacked, but on doing what they said they'd do. They were in such dire circumstances that they *did* have to ask individuals to do more with less (as the prior administrations had done), but this request had a very different flavor to it when posed by an administration that was so visibly doing the very same thing.

> *They modeled the change they wanted to see take hold throughout the organization: Figure out what your biggest priorities are today and meet them as efficiently and cost effectively as possible.*

It was a strategy that worked, and after so little had, that in itself was inspiring to the staff of BIDMC.

Leaders stayed inspired by the very notion that they could make BIDMC viable. Levy makes reference to BIDMC having gone through a "near-death experience" in the early years of its merger—and it was the "near-death" of a patient on whom tens of thousands of people depended in one way or another.

> *It seemed at times that they were inspired by the very magnitude of their endeavor.*

"Part of my job was to persuade folks that our turnaround plan could actually work, and we did that by being very open with the results," Levy told me. "Once people started to see positive results they started to believe in themselves again, and that created momentum. Once you start to do well, then you do better and better."

Infrastructure (I$_2$):

The BIDMC story is a great one to illustrate the natural flow from the creation of a shared vision, into inspiring individuals to change, and then into changing an infrastructure itself. "Throughout all of this we had to get people to work differently," Anderson reminds us, "so while we were giving them lots of support and getting their ideas, at the same time we were very clear about expectations and things that people needed to do differently."

> *"There was a pretty big change from how the place had been run in the past," says Anderson, "and there was resistance, but even with some resistance eventually it all started to happen."*

When I asked what in particular had contributed to the eventual acceptance of the need to change, Anderson continued, "I think it was just our persistence—and that we were clear. This is why we always explained *why* we had to do things the way we did."

Levy and Anderson continued to be upfront about all of the changes they intended to make at BIDMC.

"A lot of our plans made tough changes," Anderson says. "We closed things; we moved things around; we downsized some programs. These are all things that are tough to do in any organization, but particularly in academic medical centers."

As always, they sought the input of staff, created a plan that took that input into consideration, made the details of the plan available to everyone and did what they said they'd do.

Levy and Anderson harnessed the momentum of these early successes, drawing those willing to work for change more overtly into the processes—and in some cases, into leadership positions. Levy recalls that after getting information from people on the front lines, he and Anderson often asked these same individuals to continue to help keep the administration focused on what mattered most: "We often asked them to engage with us on teams and task forces to keep working on making things better."

Other staff changes were necessary as well, and those changes were tended to rather quickly. "I fired [one member of the senior management team] after a few months, and the reason she was fired was that she did not have a respectful attitude toward the doctors and the nurses, and was not willing to share information," Levy said.

When I asked Dianne Anderson about the condition of the nursing staff's middle management team upon her arrival, her answer was grim. "Actually, when I first came, I almost didn't have any [middle management team]. I pretty much had to create one. The majority of those people came from within; I only hired one or two key people from outside. I had to [fire] a couple of other people too, because they did not demonstrate the right values. Interestingly enough, they professed these values, but didn't really have them."

> *"For me the shorthand is if you don't trust the people you're working with," says Levy, "either you're in the wrong place or they are."*

I asked Anderson about the degree to which the nursing programs, which had differed so significantly at the premerger hospitals, had merged by the time she got there. "When I first got here, we still had people talking about 'are they from BI or the Deaconess?'" Anderson said. "One thing that helped was that we moved a major part of the campus over to the other campus. So we forced a lot of the blending. But we had to do a lot of work on standardization and things like that—everything from supplies to how different office procedures were done."

When I asked Anderson about BIDMC's current nursing care delivery model, she spoke of a model that truly embraces the best of what existed at both Beth Israel and New England Deaconess. "We're focused very much on a team," Anderson told me. "We still have elements of a Primary Nursing environment, but we're really focused very much on a team culture." (Note: BIDMC's "team" focus has little in common with the task-focused "team nursing" model dominant in the 1960s and '70s, but is instead a patient-focused model with a high level of interdependence between caregivers.) "We actually have done a lot of leading-edge things around team training and team dynamics across the medical center. That's very much what we are focusing on now as we go forward."

Anderson takes apparent satisfaction in pointing out that the culture of partnering with staff has been permanently integrated into the infrastructure at BIDMC. "We do these town hall meetings all the time," she says. "It's just the way that we work here."

"It's so different now, though," Anderson points out, "because we'll have meetings with staff and we'll still get issues and problems, but they are usually more about challenges having to do with our growing so much!"

Education (E₁):

Right from the start, Levy and Anderson chose all of their educational offerings for their ability to advance their ever-evolving vision of BIDMC as a world-class academic hospital.

Anderson told me, "We really had to do a lot of development with managers. About a year ago we completed a year-long process of development—almost like a mini-MBA course—for the nurse managers because a lot of them really didn't have those [management] skills; they just didn't have that background."

Because Levy and Anderson knew that a world-class hospital could be run only by world-class managers at *all levels of the organization*, they offered a variety of educational opportunities designed to help all practitioners really *feel* like world-class practitioners.

Among their trickier educational challenges were those pertaining to the culture of the organization. The culture of BIDMC in the early days of its merger was one in which many practitioners were actually *afraid* to practice like empowered professionals. "The nurses and nurse managers had been trained not to take risks," Levy said. "Under the previous initial post-merger administration if you tried to be creative or to take risks you would get slapped down." But rather than being disheartened by this aspect of BIDMC's culture, Levy and Anderson found a solution.

Anderson addressed the need for a good clear look at some of the past successes of both organizations with a visit from health care consultant Tim Porter-O'Grady. "I think that was a major turning point in unifying the two nursing staffs. We really did some work with everybody around 'leaving the old, and creating the new,' while remembering the values and successes of both organizations."

"I think the staff started to see that their new leaders were going to create something different," says Anderson, "but something that would still respect the values of the original two hospitals."

I asked Anderson whether there were other educational offerings to the staff that helped them to accept the changes and move from the pain of the merger to where they are now. Anderson was effusive in her response: "Oh, a lot of things, a tremendous number of things. We had education for staff in all areas. We provided tuition assistance, we had various educational awards, we provided education around quality, and safety—all kinds of things. We provided—and *still* provide—a tremendous amount of support for education and development."

Evidence (E_2):

Because of the "near-death experience" of BIDMC itself, great care was taken to measure its recovery. It seems that early on, Levy and Anderson measured most closely the two things they put the greatest share of their energies into managing: 1) patient satisfaction, which they addressed by removing as many barriers as possible to their staff's ability to provide quality care, and 2) reversing the tide of the organization's financial losses.

I asked Levy if there was a moment when he knew that BIDMC wasn't just surviving anymore, but that it was positioned to thrive. "We started to see it right away," he said. "We started to see improvement within weeks; virtually every quarter we were ahead of budget. We also started to see improvement in the patient satisfaction surveys we do, which is a direct reflection of how satisfied the nurses are. Because if nurses are happy, patients are happy."

As BIDMC's vision of itself as a world-class hospital evolved, the full scope of what would ultimately constitute BIDMC's success began to emerge as well.

The elements of what it meant to be a world-class hospital surfaced bit by bit, and BIDMC selected what data it would measure based on that data's ability to help the organization understand the extent to which its vision for itself was in place. They measured all relevant changes and published all results.

Though they never had a vision statement per se—one that listed all of the elements they knew must be in place in order to know they'd reached their goal—as each success came down the line, the organization's Vision for Change and its Evidence (E_2) element were built simultaneously.

> **As part of its culture of transparency, Levy and Anderson shared the evidence of every measurable change that occurred in the organization, and right from the start, the news was good.**

I left my conversation with Paul Levy and Dianne Anderson with a few impressions that reach beyond the words they spoke. In talking about the details of the BIDMC turnaround, they tend to talk mostly about the "nuts and bolts" of making things happen every day. But I feel compelled to share my own observations here about what I perceived beyond what was said.

I was struck by the way both Levy and Anderson seemed to position themselves within the organization. While any org-chart would rightly have placed them at the head of the organization, it was clear to me that *they placed themselves in a position to serve those who serve patients*. They spoke with what seemed like awe about the people they found in the organization when they arrived. And while one may reasonably assume that it was their sympathy for the abused BIDMC staff that touched them so deeply, it becomes obvious pretty quickly that it was not sympathy, but admiration that both humbled and inspired them.

Despite all of their sincere personal modesty, it is obvious that they are justifiably proud of what BIDMC has become. As they spoke of the organization it was apparent to me that in the early days, though they saw clearly every barrier, every impediment, and every sorrow that kept the organization from thriving, they also maintained a strong belief in the innate viability of the organization. They maintained belief that when they freed it from the steel trap it was caught in, it would limp for a short time, then walk, and eventually run. When they talk about "getting out of the way" of those who care for patients, they allude to the fact that what happens at the point of care is what matters most in any health care organization, and that everything they did in getting BIDMC back on its feet was ultimately to support the point of care experience of every patient and family that enters their organization.

Most of us who are privileged to lead change in organizations will do so in environments that are not as embattled as BIDMC was when Levy and Anderson got there. For practical reasons, I share the story of BIDMC's merger because it demonstrates so clearly the way in which I_2E_2 is hard at work guiding any successful change—whether those leading that change are conscious of it or not. But for personal reasons, I also share this story because it inspires me so deeply that I was certain it would inspire you too.

PART
IV

I_2E_2 in Practice

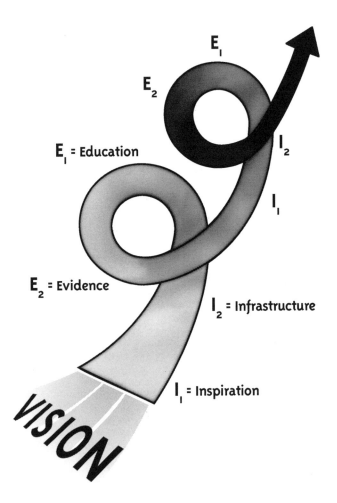

E_1

E_2

E_1 = Education

I_2

I_1

E_2 = Evidence

I_2 = Infrastructure

I_1 = Inspiration

VISION

7

Asking the Right Questions

". . . Through our assumptions and choices of methods we largely create the world we later discover."

(Cooperrider and Srivastva, 1987)

When organizations embark on major change, it is essential to bring to light as much information as possible on "where we are now" before making even the most cursory moves toward "where we want to go." As a leader of organizational change for the past two decades, I've used a method of assessment that blends Strategic Questioning and Appreciative Inquiry to help individuals figure out both where they are now *and* where they want to go.

In practice, Strategic Questioning (SQ) and Appreciative Inquiry (AI) are so complementary it can be difficult to discern their differences. But parsing their differences may help us understand how they work so well together.

While this chapter does describe what each discipline offers individually, its main purpose is to show how a combination of SQ and AI offers both the assumptions and the methodology to help us (as Cooperrider and Srivastva suggest) "create the world we want to discover."

Strategic Questioning

The gift of Strategic Questioning is its ability to provoke generative thinking.

Social activist Fran Peavey has long been an authority on the art of Strategic Questioning, conducting workshops on developing strategic questioning techniques and employing the techniques herself in her work for social change. In an article called *Strategic Questioning: An Experiment in Communication of the Second Kind* (Peavy, 2003), Peavey shows us that strategic questions have the power to take us beyond the static realm of right and wrong answers into the kind of generative thinking that helps us create changes that represent our deepest, most authentic desires. Strategic Questions engage others by asking them to actively consider an unlimited number of options—something we are far too rarely invited to do, and something few of us think to do when not specifically invited to do so.

Peavey reminds us that most of us learned in school that there is a right answer and a wrong answer. (It is likely that if we ever concluded that 4 X 5 = 25, we were corrected, rather than led into a discussion of how we had arrived at our conclusion, which might possibly have created in us a better understanding of how multiplication works.) We have been trained to think of answers in terms of right and wrong and we tend to behave as though there are two sides to every issue—but no more than two.

Questioning that helps us find the "right" answer is not generative, as it only helps us to find something that is already known. Similarly, looking at only two choices limits our decision making. As neither leads us beyond what is known, both essentially encourage us to make the same choices we've always made.

Strategic Questions engage us in creating theories, plans for change and bridges between where we are now and where we want to be.

One of Peavey's favorite strategic questions begins, "What would it take for you to . . . ?" In the context of a health care organization transitioning to Relationship-Based Care, for example, this question could go something like this: "What would it take for you to make your own practice 100% relationship-based?" This question opens us to a discussion of how to build the bridge necessary to get where we want to go, and perhaps even more importantly it voices the assumption that building that bridge is possible. The very question itself stimulates thought, opens possibilities, generates ideas and moves our planning forward.

Strategic questions ask:

- How would our new model of care be experienced by patients, families, staff, physicians, executives, trustees and our community?

- What in our current culture deserves to move with us into our future?

- What will it take to transform our organization into what we desire it to be?

These questions invite people into generative, expansive visioning.

Peavey does not imply, however, that strategic questioning is the only kind of questioning that has value. To accomplish comprehensive change, we must first get a feel for the terrain, so Peavey encourages the use of a number of different sorts of questions with which to lay the groundwork for effective Strategic Questioning. It serves no one for agents of change to go into a situation assuming the worst—that they will meet resistance; that people in the organization are not already engaging in satisfying, inspiring practice; that the organization is failing or needs "fixing". Instead, useful assessment requires objective questioning that helps agents of change get a clear picture not only of what really is happening in an organization, but of how and why its successes have been possible.

Strategic questioning is designed to uncover the deep desires of the heart.

These desires play an important role in organization-wide initiatives like the transformation to Relationship-Based Care. Despite appearances to the contrary, substantive change doesn't enter an organization through its board and executive offices. It enters an organization through each individual practitioner, and it takes its most meaningful expression at the point of care. This means that it's essential to engage every individual in the organization at the heart level.

It's not the organization that will be embarking on change, after all; it's the people.

Strategic Questioning methods help us unearth the information about our organizations that will do us the most good in our future. If we can bring what we are best at into the light, we can then harness the energy of our past and current excellence to help pull our new endeavor forward. The questions we use to uncover that core of excellence must be both strategic and appreciative.

Appreciative Inquiry

The gift of Appreciative Inquiry is its ability to focus us on our proven strengths, a prelude to imaging our desired future.

Appreciative Inquiry is accomplished in four steps:

1. Participants are asked to describe a positive experience they have had, related to the current opportunity for change.

2. Participants are asked to identify what success factors contributed to the previously lived positive experience.

3. Participants are asked to consider what it would take to generate an increase in similar positive experiences in the desired environment of the future.

4. Participants are finally asked to formulate a provocative statement of their desired future environment—worded in concrete terms, as if it is already happening.

Appreciative Inquiry starts with a Strategic Question.

When asking individuals to describe a previously lived positive experience, we invite them to delve into a comprehensive exploration of something at which they have proven successful. They are encouraged to expand their understanding of something they once created in hopes of creating more of it in the future. Thus AI informs both strategic and operational action planning. Appreciative Inquiry sessions always begin with a values-laden question like:

- What can you tell us about your most memorable experience of when a patient's or family's number one expressed need was met?

- Please describe a time when you were struck by the high quality of collaboration with which your care team worked.

- Please describe a period in your career in which you felt you took excellent care of yourself while continuing to provide high quality care for your patients.

Each of these questions is deliberately leading, as it intends to draw participants into a discussion only of experiences at which they have already proven themselves successful, and which are consistent with the organization's vision and mission. This reminds everyone involved that what we are hoping to create is no more difficult or elusive than anything we've created already.

> *Appreciative Inquiry's overriding message is "We've done it before, and we can do more of it now."*

While the core of Appreciative Inquiry is its ability to focus us on what is working well rather than what is going wrong in any given situation, it has another nuance that bears exploration at this point. Appreciative Inquiry directs us away from considering problems-as-problems and toward *envisioning* what we want to accomplish irrespective of any problems that may exist. It does not ignore real barriers that may exist. It chooses to focus on what's worked, thus positioning participants to engage in creating an optimal future.

> *Considering problems as such limits our thinking to solutions directly related to solving those narrowly defined problems.*

For example, if we determine that one problem in a health care organization is that staff are dissatisfied with their schedules, the identified problem directs us to put our focus on scheduling rather than opening us to possibilities for larger, more systemic change. With a focus on problems, we perpetuate a model in which problems arise, problems are examined, and problems are solved; but it's a model in which the broader system from which these problems emerged remains largely unexamined. Delving deeper using Appreciative Inquiry might help us to see that what people really want is a sense of meaning in what they do. It is possible that when a more visionary goal is identified, the "problem" of dissatisfaction with schedules falls away completely. Focusing on problems has a narrowing effect on our thinking. It is not generative—it does not inspire us to generate new paradigms or ways of being.

In the field, AI would guide us to ask this staff to remember a time when their work schedules were consistent with their patients' lengths of stay and their personal life balance. Strategic Questioning would offer us the words to start our AI exercise with a values-laden, generative question that inspires broad, creative thinking about the very nature of how the staff functions within their unit—and by extension within the organization. The Appreciative Inquiry that follows would ask the group to identify what contributed to their past successes with scheduling. We'd then ask a strategic question like "What would it take to recreate an even better version of that past success in our current environment?"

One thought on the topic of schedules has expanded to include a broad consideration of the very way in which staff function within their environment, a clear vision for a desired future begins to emerge.

While Appreciative Inquiry leads us first to look at what we ourselves say, it is also of benefit to listen to what *others* say with an ear for Appreciative Inquiry. It is possible, of course, for you to frame your issue in entirely appreciative terms and for those you are talking with to remain problem-focused while listening to you. If it is their longtime habit or personal dynamic to do so, they may grab hold of whatever "problem" they can identify in what you've said and run with it. If, for example, you are in the middle of an exercise of Appreciative Inquiry and somebody says, "That will never work, we've tried that," the other person has revealed that he or she has previous related experience and is aware of potential barriers to success. Gentle persistence is required in your efforts to elicit favorable past experiences from which further exploration will follow . . . without giving ground to potentially negative discourse that leads us back to the status quo. The goal is always to bring the conversation back to generative, visionary levels of thinking and creating.

> **Strategic Questioning and Appreciative Inquiry invite people into the creative process so overtly that it prevents the perception that the changes we are working to create are just a cleverly disguised mandated overlay program.**

Each question we ask is designed to take thinkers beyond a narrow problems-focus into a broader envisioning of a desired future—together.

What Strategic Questioning and Appreciative Inquiry have in common is the way in which they help us direct our focus. Neither allows its user to be distracted by a "problem" of any kind. Therefore, Strategic Questioning mixed with Appreciative Inquiry is the perfect formula for growth. In addition to these methods, World Café and Dynamic Dialogue have been effective in making meaningful conversation possible at all levels of organizations during change.

In designing your action plans, use these tools throughout the entire design, implementation and sustaining phases. If you use them long enough for them to become your lifelong habit, so much the better.

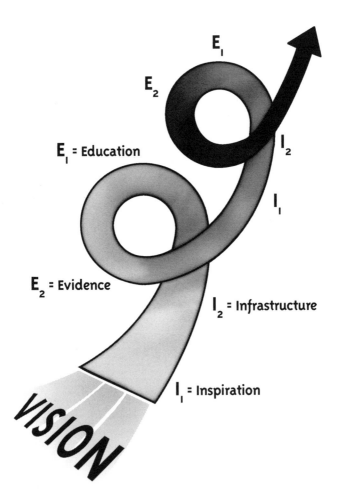

E~I~

E~2~

E~I~ = Education

E~2~ = Evidence

I~2~

I~I~

I~2~ = Infrastructure

I~I~ = Inspiration

VISION

8

Implementing Large-Scale Change: Relationship-Based Care Scenario

The example threaded through this chapter addresses information specific to the implementation of Relationship-Based Care (RBC) in a health care setting, but the example itself is helpful for those wishing to lead *any* organization-wide change. This chapter features both an example of the completed action plan itself and some of the questioning that inspired the items that were determined essential to the plan. Remember, since every organization is unique it would not work to simply adopt a ready-made action plan, so I encourage you to read the material pertaining to how the items were arrived at as well as the items themselves. If for quick reference later you wish to peruse just the action plan itself, you will see that it appears in bold print throughout the chapter.

Relationship-Based Care is a patient-focused care delivery culture embraced in health care facilities around the world. Its central concept is that each patient's care is managed by a Registered Nurse for the patient's entire length of stay on a particular unit, and the patient and family work with a consistent care team who proactively communicate all pertinent information about the patient's care with care team members, physicians and staff. The patient's goals and individual needs drive care decisions. RBC has been found to greatly enhance staff and patient satisfaction as well as the coordination of care.

A Relationship-Based Care culture includes a healing, caring environment within which focused attention has been made to:

- strengthen leadership at all levels
- enhance collaboration and partnerships
- professionalize practice
- maximize resource utilization
- streamline care delivery in ways that support professional practice
- measure salient patient, staff, physician, and other organizational outcomes related to work redesign and specific to RBC

The implementation of Relationship-Based Care is a comprehensive cultural change that will influence nearly everything anyone in an organization does from the boardroom to the bedside.

While RBC may initially be proposed by an organization's Chief Nursing Officer, it comes to full flower in the boardroom before any of it makes its way to the bedside. It becomes the center of every mission, vision and values statement; and it becomes the touchstone for decision making at all levels.

After an organization's intention to make a pervasive cultural change is firmly rooted at the executive level—as is evidenced by its formulation of a comprehensive, clearly articulated vision—it is time to create an action plan for changes at the patient care and support services level. The following is an example of how I_2E_2—with its systematic and systemic consideration of the Inspiration (I_1), Infrastructure (I_2), Education (E_1) and Evidence (E_2) necessary to create sustained change—can be used to implement and sustain RBC in a health care organization.

Relationship-Based Care Scenario

A hospital-wide vision statement, while serving the valuable function of shaping an organization's identity, is rarely, if ever, instructive at a behavioral level. Vision, values and mission statements are intended to point the way; they are strategic directives. Translating these directives into tangible, practical behaviors requires visioning by individuals and departments throughout the organization. *These* visions become unit standards of practice, reaching tangibly into the individual behaviors of all practitioners.

When a fully integrated cultural change is desired to bring a vision to life, it is necessary to take action on an operational level before tactical action plans can be implemented at the unit level. When the vision is valued by all stakeholders, a common purpose becomes known and the knowledge of a shared focus unifies everyone around this valued purpose—in this example, Relationship-Based Care.

The RBC principles that follow include tangible operating guidelines to help create a cohesive implementation throughout the organization. These principles serve as the bridge between the organizational vision, mission and values statements and the individual and collective departmental action plans. While each unit and department will ultimately translate the vision and principles into action plans unique to their clinical environment, the composite vision establishes a solid framework within which that adaptation can happen. Notice also that the vision for change is worded as though the desired change is already in place. The creation of a successful vision for change is always done with the mindset that the change is already alive and well within the organization. The vision statement is worded such that it carries the energy that created it.

Operational Care Delivery Vision—RBC Principles:

- Each patient's care is managed by one RN who establishes a therapeutic relationship at (or soon after) admission, and this relationship lasts throughout the patient's stay on the care unit.

- The patient-nurse relationship is not disrupted by assignment.

- The patient and family are actively engaged in the development of a care plan driven by their expressed wishes.

- The plan of care is mutually determined within the patient, family, nurse and physician partnership.

- Patient care resources are available, functional and efficient.

- Care is attentive to the mind, body and spirit.

- The patient experiences caring as he or she describes caring upon admission.

- Patient, staff and physician satisfaction scores increase, and all fiscal and staff retention targets are met.

- The patient and family are satisfied because they believe that their number one expressed concern regarding this episode of care is also the number one priority for their RN and the health care team.

This action-oriented "vision for change" creates a focal point for every future action in the patient care services division. It is a clear statement of who we intend to *be* in relation to our patients and their families and our staff in the day-to-day. It is a statement that defines a desired future to which the entire organization will aspire.

The operational vision for change answers the question "Where will we specifically focus our efforts in implementing the Relationship-Based Care model?"

In the following four sections, an action plan unfolds revealing the Inspiration (I_1), Infrastructure (I_2), Education (E_1) and Evidence (E_2) necessary to bring this RBC vision to life at the patient care level.

To see a Gantt chart showing the first year of this action plan, see Appendix B (page 177).

The I_2E_2 Action Plan:

Inspiration:

Inspiration comes from appreciating past successes, acknowledging the valuable contributions we've made and staying focused on our vision for an even better future.

When implementing RBC, we can begin to shape our insight regarding Inspiration (I_1) opportunities by asking ourselves questions like:

- What are the benefits of the new vision for our patients and their families?

- What do we as individual health care prac-titioners stand to gain if we change our practice?

- What favorable impact will this change have on our physicians?

- What do we as an organization stand to gain if we change our practice?

- How does the community stand to benefit if we change our practice?

- What does the health care field as a whole stand to gain by our example?

As you imagine answers to the first set of questions, you will begin to think about ways to engage others whose commitment to and participation in the vision will be essential to making your vision a reality. The next set of questions gets at how to inspire *others* to personally embrace the larger vision. Consider individuals from all levels and positions within your organization.

- Who of influence may already share the new vision?

- Who has demonstrated a personal or professional inclination toward the "mindset" of the new vision?

- Who could be inspired to advance and contribute to our vision for change?

- Who could be identified as potential leaders of this change?

- Who will be primarily impacted both operationally and tactically by this change?

- How might we engage everyone in developing a shared vision?

- What will it take to inspire them to advance the new vision?

- What will it take to convince others that every individual's effort is important and will make a difference?

After you've considered how others can be brought into the plan, make your inquiry personal. Leaders are dealers of hope, and as such, your most important step when taking on the task of inspiring others is to figure out what inspires hope in *you*. Ask yourself:

- What values are most compelling in the new vision for change?

- What and who inspire me to grow and develop as a person and leader?

- What insights are sources of inspiration for me as a professional?

- How would others describe my therapeutic behaviors, my "signature" work—my unique expression of caring and healing?

- What have I done to earn the trust of those in my organization?

- What keeps me focused on patients and families despite distractions by multiple work challenges?

The points of Inspiration (I_1) you eventually include in your action plan may not be direct answers to any or all of these questions, but these questions will lead you into an important exploration of what inspires you and what might potentially inspire others. In this scenario, the items below were identified by colleagues as some of the best ways to inspire people at all levels of the organization to embrace the new Relationship-Based Care vision.

Inspiration (I_1):

I am inspired when health care professionals see patients as human beings whose lives have been disrupted by health issues, when we recognize that patients are vulnerable and when we acknowledge that patients' families often need as much or more emotional support than patients do.

I believe every one of us really cares about giving patients the very best of care. I am inspired when that is visible in our daily practice, despite heavy workloads and imperfect systems.

The implementation of RBC eliminates fragmented, automatic, task-oriented, impersonal patient care. It makes things as efficient and safe as possible for everyone and is far more rewarding for me as a professional.

Implementing RBC takes commitment, effort, creativity, persistence and leadership. Each of these is its own reward.

Caregivers are inspired and renewed by the **Reigniting the Spirit of Caring** *workshop we are offering.*

Appreciative Inquiry focus groups inspire individuals at all levels in the organization.

At least 60% of my colleagues share my values and priorities as do my manager and several of the physicians. This inspires me to maintain my focus and have confidence that we can improve our practice.

Infrastructure (I_2):

Once the operational vision for change is set and we have addressed how we intend to inspire ourselves and others to bring about our desired future, we begin to assess our organization's Infrastructure (I_2)—its strategic, operational and tactical workings—to assure that every aspect of it actively advances the new vision.

We start by looking appreciatively at the role definitions, standards, systems, practices and processes already in place to see what is working well.

We keep and augment what is working, and we redesign all that does not actively advance the vision. So that we can dig with focus into our existing roles, standards, systems, practices and processes, we again ask ourselves Strategic Questions—questions that provoke generative thinking—to help us add some tangible details to our action plan.

Questions that Address Strategic-Level Considerations:

- In what ways do your personal vision and the shared vision for change support the strategic mission and vision of the organization?

Questions that Address Operational-Level Considerations:

- What roles, standards, systems, practices and processes already in place advance the new vision? Which of these could be amended to advance the vision?

- What changes in our daily practice would increase the likelihood that this vision will *live* in daily practice?

- How will you link recommendations from the Work Complexity Assessment to the overall action plan?

- What committees or councils will be necessary to provide guidance, voice and accountability for individuals at all levels of the organization during the time of transition and beyond?

- In what ways can our committees or councils interface in support of RBC and the operational vision?

- Which work group, if any, might best serve as champions for RBC?

- What concrete caring, healing behaviors can we enhance or adopt into our clinical and leadership practice?

- What support (from individuals or groups) will we need?—and what systems, practices and processes might assure that we get it?

- What creative, innovative dialogic methods might we use to uncover deeper understanding of the infrastructure that will inform our action planning?

Questions that Address Tactical-Level Concerns:

- What specific changes in our behavior will we personally make to advance the new vision?

- How can our vision be integrated into the daily fabric of our personal lives to assure that it lives beyond now?

- What processes will we put into place to keep ourselves on our chosen path?

- To what specific collegial behaviors will we commit?

In this scenario, the following points were identified as elements of Infrastructure (I_2) that are essential for the new vision of RBC to really live in the daily functioning of the organization.

Infrastructure (I_2):

The principles of RBC, adapted and endorsed by executive nursing leadership, are disseminated to all patient care and service support department personnel.

All patients at the time of admission (or within 12 hours of admission) are selected by an RN or assigned a primary nurse who manages their care for the duration of their stay on the clinical unit. Patient-nurse relationships are not disrupted by assignment.

At admission every patient is asked, "What is your #1 need or concern regarding this episode of care?" and "What impact is this episode of care having on your life?"

At admission all patients are asked to describe the manner in which they would most appreciate receiving care; they are coached to identify what specific behaviors they want to experience.

The answers to the previous questions drive the plan of care and are shared with the health care team; the answers to these questions also feature prominently in shift and condition reports.

Quality Improvement (QI) indicators are determined to monitor the outcomes.

Staff schedules are developed with a primary goal of providing continuity of care within the parameters of balanced family life and labor agreements (i.e., staff can choose to work three consecutive days if the average length of stay on their unit is three days).

Staff assignments are made with a priority on continuity of relationships. (Continuity of caregiver relationships is a greater priority than room assignment.)

RNs proactively seek out the attending physician to collaborate on behalf of the patient's plan of care and preferably meet in the patient's room.

Supervisors report daily on the number or percentage of RN-Patient relationships that are disrupted because of reassignment, providing both rationale for the disruption and plans to prevent future disruptions.

Supervisors, nurse managers and executives who visit the unit meet each new patient (when clinically appropriate) and reinforce their intention to meet the patient's number one need and request for personalized care.

Job descriptions and performance appraisals include expectations and rewards for creative thinking, relationship management and leadership at the point of care.

Unit Practice Councils (UPCs), peer councils that guide each unit's practice as part of a "shared governance" model, establish reflective practice procedures for each shift and for monthly use on each unit.

The Results Council (the oversight council which has level-3 authority for the entire transformation to RBC) meets with UPC members to endorse and support their translation of RBC principles to their unit work environment.

Intradisciplinary reflective practice sessions are held monthly. Sessions highlight cases where a patient's number one need was met, what care the patient received, what challenges staff overcame to meet that need and any insights staff gained about what factors contributed to their success. The dialogue includes ways in which these types of exemplary experiences can be provided for an even greater number of future patients.

The Caring Model™, a customer service program, is implemented to support professional practice efforts (i.e., RBC) and provides an opportunity for all members of the organization to join in making an intentional difference for patients and their families.

The implementation of RBC principles specific to the allied health professionals and service support staff has a favorable influence on patient satisfaction.

Recruitment protocols, orientation and staff development curricula reinforce principles and practices of RBC.

Infrastructure changes often mean that people will be asked to do things they've never done before. This means they'll have knowledge and skill-building challenges that must be addressed in the next section of the I_2E_2 model—Education (E_1).

Education (E_1):

In order to determine what learning initiatives will be necessary for those in the organization who are taking on significant changes, consider what changes are being introduced in light of the current knowledge and skill levels in your organization.

If you identify knowledge or skill level gaps, you will implement learning initiatives to fill those gaps.

To assess the educational needs of the whole organization, you'll ask:

- What learning programs already in place advance the RBC vision?

- What knowledge and skill-building will individuals and teams need in order to adopt and *sustain* the desired vision?

- How will staff members, leaders, physicians, trustees and others acquire the knowledge and skills necessary to advance this change?

- How might employees at various levels in the organization mentor or support each other?

- What is the full scope of what staff members need to know to provide relationship-based patient and family care?

- How can we help staff develop and grow their critical and creative thinking skills?

- How can we help staff develop and grow their relationship management skills?

- How can we help staff develop and grow their leadership knowledge and skills?

- How can RBC concepts become integrated into the recruitment and orientation of new hires?

Then inquire about what educational initiatives might benefit you and others on the leadership team. Ask yourself:

- What do I need to know to enhance my ability to achieve my vision as a leader?

- What more do I need to know to lead the RBC implementation process? How will I acquire this knowledge?

- Who might support *me?* Is there a role model I could invite into a mentoring relationship?

- What is the full scope of what I need to know to achieve my personal vision for providing excellent patient and family care?

- What will I do to develop and grow my creative thinking, relationship management and leadership knowledge and skills?

The following are the points identified as essential for the hospital in our scenario to add to the education section of its action plan.

Education (E_1):

*Leadership reviews State Practice Acts for nurses,
allied health professionals and support staff
in order to clarify implications for maximizing the
contributions of support staff (LPNs and CNAs in
particular) and strengthening the role of the RN.*

*We study findings related to caring and healing
environments, patient preferences and models of
care delivery that support professional practice.*

*Creative/critical thinking skill-building experiences
are provided for everyone in the organization.*

*Relationship management skill-building experiences
are provided for everyone in the organization.*

*Everyone in the organization is provided with
leadership skill-building experiences, including*
Leading an Empowered Organization *for all
executives and frontline managers and* **Leadership
at the Point of Care** *for all nurses and
allied health professionals.*

Evidence (E₂):

In the next section, we consider what evidence will show us that we are succeeding. When constructing the Evidence (E_2) element of your action plan, check what you are measuring against your vision statement to ensure that you are collecting evidence—point by point—on every aspect of what you intend to create. Our Evidence (E_2) element shows us how far we've come and how far we still have to go.

The following questions address what evidence we might collect on the functioning of the organization as a whole:

- How will we demonstrate or measure a persistent focus on the vision for change (organizationally, departmentally and individually)?

- How will we demonstrate RBC's actual impact, considering both process and outcomes measures?

- How will we measure the quality perceptions of patients, staff and physicians, particularly satisfaction and loyalty?

- How will we measure the clinical factors of morbidity, mortality and patient safety relative to our specific patient population?

- How will we measure the fiscal benefits of RBC as they pertain to staff retention, physician recruitment, vacancy rate and average caregiver salary cost per adjusted patient day?

- How will we capture and report on the impact of specific RBC principles implemented on discrete patient units?

- What behaviors, outcomes or tangible changes would provide evidence that we are moving toward the vision for change?

- What mechanism will we enact to track our progress?

- How will we periodically measure and celebrate our persistent commitment and focus on progressing to achieve the vision for change?

- How will we measure the extent to which our inspirational efforts have been successful?

- How will we measure the extent to which our educational initiatives have been successful?

- How will we measure the extent to which evidence collected in response to the vision for change is being used to create further inspiration for those involved?

- How will we know when our desired future is a reality?

Now again, make your inquiry personal. Ask yourself

- How will I measure the persistence of my own focus on the overall vision for change?
- How will I measure the extent to which my efforts to stay inspired really are successful?
- How will I measure the extent to which my own learning initiatives have been successful?

The following are the points of Evidence (E₂) the hospital in our example has identified as essential in its transition to Relationship-Based Care:

Evidence (E₂):

All shift reports, staff meetings, and leadership meetings begin with a story highlighting the way a patient's number one stated priority was met.

Unit Practice Councils translate the RBC Principles into action plans for their unique clinical area.

"Moments of excellence" are celebrated spontaneously by staff and managers. Attention is focused on what was done right and what it would take to bring the same type of experiences to an even greater number of patients.

Patient, staff and physician satisfaction scores all increase. Staff retention targets are met.

Patient clinical quality scores improve.

Organizational fiscal targets are met—particularly those related to human resources.

Process indicator measures validate that infrastructure changes are in place—addressing how care is delivered as well as the results or impact of that care. They measure:

1) The percentage of patients discharged each week who have experienced the nurse-patient relationship as described in the operational vision statement.

2) The percentage of patients admitted who were selected by or assigned to an RN within 12 hours of their arrival.

3) The average number of patient
stays during which the nurse-patient
relationship is not disrupted by
assignment or re-assignment.

4) The average number of times during
a patient's stay that his or her number
one need or concern is shared during
shift report.

**Operational documents (job descriptions,
performance appraisals, reward standards) reflect
integration of RBC principles.**

You will notice a direct correlation between our
Evidence (E_2) element and our Operational Care Delivery Vision Statement. We measure everything that
we desire to create, because we know that everything
that is measured gets managed.

While it would seem, since we have cycled through
the entire I_2E_2 model, that our scenario has come to
an end, it hasn't.

**Once we have determined that our vision for RBC is
a reality—alive and well within our organization—
we turn our attention toward deepening
and sustaining that vision.**

Remember that in I_2E_2, all evidence collected is then used to inspire everyone to stay focused on the newly integrated cultural change. Once we complete one cycle of tending to the Inspiration (I_1), Infrastructure (I_2), Education (E_1) and Evidence (E_2) of our current action plan, we devise another action plan (typically a refinement of the original, taking subsequent changes into consideration) and cycle through all four elements again.

Please note: *As I stated at the beginning of this chapter, the examples in this chapter represent only a partial—and very generic—list of items that may be included in an I_2E_2 action plan for change on the operational level. In real-world situations, each organization adopts and adapts the principles of RBC in its own unique way. The examples provided here are only meant to help illustrate what an action plan can look like and to stimulate thought on what an organization might wish to include in an I_2E_2 action plan for transition to RBC.*

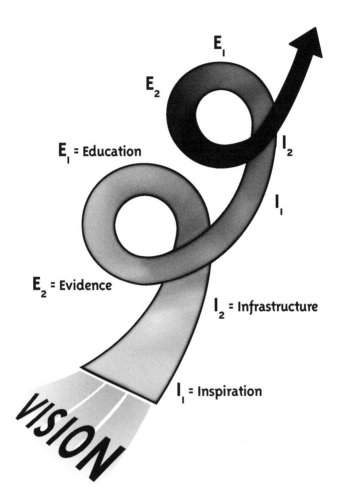

E_1

E_2

E_1 = Education

I_2

I_1

E_2 = Evidence

I_2 = Infrastructure

I_1 = Inspiration

VISION

9

Strategies for Sustaining Change

As is stated throughout this book, inspiration comes not from identifying problems, but from recounting our successes and then committing to a vision of how we want things to be. As inspiration is one of the primary keys to sustainability, it follows that sustainability is supported not by identifying, cataloging or focusing on problems, but by focusing continually and *dynamically* on our progress toward our shared vision for a desired future.

In the old problems-focused mindset, departments pulled together in a crisis, but often fell apart when things improved. Sustainability depends partly, of course, upon our ability to function well together when the going is tough, but we in health care have been good at that for a long time. We're used to working with people in crisis. We're used to working under pressure, with limited resources, in life-or-death situations. It's when things start going *well* that we sometimes lose our focus.

We might assume logically that either complacency or the distraction of multiple new challenges, mandates or ideas is responsible for the derailments we experience when circumstances improve. But for those of us in health care, it is more likely that we are just too busy to ponder (much less plan for) changing all that would need to be changed. Once we leave the old model of "find-a-problem-and-solve-it" and become comfortable *envisioning* things as we want them to be, there is no limit to what we can accomplish.

> *Focusing entirely on a vision of how you want things to be is so exhilarating that you'll never want to go back to the days of figuring out what's wrong with your organization and putting all of your time and attention into fixing it.*

Focusing on problems puts us on the defensive; it saps our energies, and it can even pit us against one another. The problems-focused mindset also makes accountability a tricky issue. Think about it—if we are discussing problems and then asking individuals to stand up and be accountable, accountability in that context is tantamount to blame.

If we are discussing past successes and our vision for the future, and then asking individuals to stand up and be accountable, accountability becomes the gateway to empowerment.

It has long been automatic for most of us to see a problem as something deserving our immediate attention and persistent focus. We stay focused on our problems until we can see that they are solved. Following our visions to their logical conclusions, however, can take some rethinking—especially when we throw in the notion that this week's pursuit of our vision may inspire some *new* ways for us to pursue our vision next week. This is particularly true in a work environment as complex as health care.

Fortunately, unlike the draining pursuit of problems, the pursuit of a shared vision for change is energizing. Perhaps that's why just about every statement of mission, vision or values is really a collection of aspirations that, taken together, create the inspiration for action.

The cyclical nature of I_2E_2 helps us stay focused on our vision for change—continually.

As stated earlier, once we complete one cycle of tending to the Inspiration (I_1), Infrastructure (I_2), Education (E_1) and Evidence (E_2) of our current action plan, we devise action plan after action plan and cycle through all four elements again and again.

Consider for a moment the earlier scenario in this section on implementing Relationship-Based Care in a health care setting. If the organization had been working from the assumption that RBC was intended to address the organization's problems, once RBC was "in place" (the reality of which is objectively verifiable) their work would be finished. But their vision is for RBC to live and thrive in their organization indefinitely. I_2E_2 provides the structure for sustaining the changes we bring to our organizations.

Sustaining Group Energy

When you are part of an organization undergoing substantive change, you have the tactical action plans of several groups to concern yourself with on an ongoing basis. In an organization implementing changes using I_2E_2, you have ready access to a formula for keeping those action plans relevant and useful for as long as you wish.

Strategic-level groups ensure that what's actually happening in the organization is aligned with its mission, vision and values.

On the strategic level—the level of organization-wide thinking and action planning—it is customary to revisit all mission, vision and values statements periodically. After the conclusion of the first cycle of I_2E_2, once the executive team and board members see their strategic plans in action, they will use Appreciative Inquiry to assess the ways in which their stated mission, vision and values reflect what is actually happening in the organization. They will then bridge any gaps between the vision for change and what is proving both possible and desirable in the organization.

Just as each organization is unique, so is every department or unit within an organization. The beauty of this plan is its inclusive feature that honors the talents of individuals, the unique patient populations, and the practice environments inherent in acute and chronic care facilities. It does so while providing a cohesive blueprint overall, so synergy is created and experienced.

While strategic visions remain fairly constant, operational and tactical visions and action plans are appropriately dynamic and allow for future innovations.

For example, if your original I_2E_2 plan for the implementation of Relationship-Based Care included the principle, "Every patient will experience a therapeutic relationship with an RN beginning at the time of admission" (which is a reasonable expectation on most units in some hospitals), but it is discovered after a cycle of I_2E_2 that it is impractical for some units in your organization to achieve this, the staff may amend their tactical vision. It might read, "Every patient will experience a therapeutic relationship with one RN beginning at the time of admission, or within 12 hours of admission."

While I_2E_2 helps us to design comprehensive, inclusive, well thought-out plans for change, no plan is perfect. A meaningful revisit to your most recent I_2E_2 action plan on a cyclical basis is necessary for sustaining the energy of the strategic group.

The Results Council, or Oversight Team, models this behavior through its monthly agenda. Each functional subgroup routinely reports the current status against the overall two-year plan, describes what activities are imminent and engages the entire council in a dialogue around plan enhancements. The conversation and focus is always forward and upward.

Department-level groups will help keep planning meaningful in the organization's department and units.

On the department level—the level of planning that affects departments, teams and units within the organization—every aspect of the original I_2E_2 plan should be periodically revisited to determine whether its elements have been successfully implemented as well as whether any of the original elements in the plan have proven unworkable, unnecessary or inadvertently counterproductive.

In implementing RBC, Unit Practice Councils (UPCs) are established to assist in everything from the initial design of the unit's vision and action plan, to its implementation, and right into its sustaining phases. When you've cycled through I_2E_2 once, the UPC's work is largely the verification and celebration of your successful efforts. They are the body responsible for taking evidence of past success and using it to keep their units laser-focused on their vision for change.

The World Café practice of engaging participants in meaningful yet casual conversation around questions of value and purpose has been quite successful on several levels. It's been useful in introducing RBC to nurses, physicians, trustees, executives and managers new to the facility. It's been effective in facilitating conversations between community leaders and professionals. And World Café can serve as the innovative vehicle to broaden and deepen the knowledge of successes related to RBC implementation when leaders at the point of care assemble to share their stories about what really worked, why it worked and what more they expect to accomplish.

Sustaining Individual Energy

The two factors that nearly always determine whether or not changes prove sustainable are the commitment level and commensurate actions of each individual involved in sustaining the change. Therefore, as always, the commitment level of the larger group is best addressed by first working on *individual* commitment. If you intend to lead and sustain change in your organization, your own commitment to your vision must be rock solid.

I$_2$E$_2$ can help you formulate your own personal plan to stay committed to your organization's vision for change.

The cyclical structure of the I$_2$E$_2$ model is the key to using it to sustain change in individual as well as organizational realms. At set points throughout the duration of a project, ask yourself questions about your own ongoing experience of the Inspiration (I$_1$), Infrastructure (I$_2$), Education (E$_1$) and Evidence (E$_2$) initiatives. These questions might include:

Vision *Where are we currently (on a scale of 1-10 with 10 as the ideal) toward our goal of achieving an RBC culture?* What will it take to achieve the next level of RBC in our organization? How will the achievement of that next step be experienced by patients, families, staff and physicians?

(I_1) *What inspires me most about this transformation process?* What inspired me about this project in the first place? What new inspirations have emerged for me since the implementation began?

(I_2) *What can I alter in my day-to-day practice to advance the new vision now?* Can I personally make a more impactful contribution to promoting the new vision? (Think of both words and deeds.) In what ways do these practices validate excellence in my job performance or help me to be consistent with our organization's mission?

(E_1) *What additional education would benefit me most now?* Am I adequately prepared to take on the current or next phase in this project? What new intellectual, behavioral or functional capacities might I expand or acquire?

(E_2) *What measurements can I put into place to provide evidence of my personal contribution in promoting the new vision now?* Am I actively using that evidence to inspire me in this project? What measurable impact have I made for patients, their families and my colleagues?

These questions might help the administrator in our example of implementing Relationship-Based Care to prepare a personal I_2E_2 plan like the one below.

Vision:

I successfully lead the implementation of Relationship-Based Care in my organization. I remain committed to ensuring that RBC principles are evident within every department, unit, team and individual in the organization and that all quality goals are met within the established timelines.

Inspiration (I_1):

I stay inspired to lead this change because RBC has been proven to contribute to both patient satisfaction and clinical quality. I am inspired by every success I see in the organization. Our most inspiring successes to date are that in the first 12 months of implementation

- patient satisfaction scores rose from 11% to 89%;

- turnover has decreased from 30% to 4%;
- there is a waiting list for RNs seeking employment in three clinical areas; and
- our market share has grown by 10%.

I am equally inspired by the sense of partnership that I experience among my colleagues and in work-groups. The harmony is palpable.

Infrastructure (I_2):

I commit to making a tactical shift in how I talk about the initiative to bring RBC to the organization. I recommit my efforts to be positive in every conversation I have about it with *anyone*, inside or outside of the organization.

I'm very vision-focused while talking to groups of stakeholders about this project, but I'm sometimes problems-focused when I talk about it in one-to-one conversations.

I continue to introduce discrete concepts from the RBC book and LEO program each month at staff meetings.

I refine the monthly report I provide to my supervisor to more clearly focus on successful applications of the RBC implementation.

Education (E_1):

I reread *Good to Great*, by Jim Collins. It reminds me that modeling enthusiastic support for RBC helps me to lead better—and feel better!

I also review *Exuberance: The Passion for Life*, by Kay Redfield Jamison, and aspire to be seen by others as joyfully exuberant.

Evidence (E_2):

My colleagues acknowledge my successful switch to consistent positive language and support for the change process.

Additional evidence of my persistent focus on the vision is seen in the staff meeting minutes illustrating RBC and LEO concepts; the developmental learning plan created in partnership with the educational department; and the organization's investment in the *Relationships at the Point of Care* program for RNs and support staff to launch year two of our RBC implementation.

This exercise reminds me over and over why I'm involved in the project—it is in 100% alignment with the reason I got into health care in the first place. (It's something I've put in my planner to do the day before any major meeting related to this project.)

Without an exercise like the one above, leaders may think creatively about changes that affect the whole organization without ever thinking about what changes they can make in their own more personal day-to-day practices.

As Robert Schuller said,
"If it is to be, it is up to me."

I_2E_2 helps us to look comprehensively at our own practices. As in the example of the administrator who commits to being more positive in one-to-one conversations about the change he or she is leading, we too, as individuals in an organization undergoing change, can look at our own daily practice (using I_2E_2 to ensure that we look into every nook and cranny) and reassess those practices to determine whether we can bring them into closer alignment with the organization's vision for change. No action that advances the overall vision for change is too small—or too *personal*—to be of value to the organization. Even if your personal contribution in any given moment is only to speak well of any aspect of the change, value that contribution.

The keys to sustaining any new vision for change are persistent focus, dogged determination, resiliency, continuity and the integration of the individual efforts that specifically advance that vision.

This continuity of effort requires constancy of both focus and commitment. True commitment starts with *self* and then moves out to relationships with others—patients, their families, colleagues, our own family members and so on. With I_2E_2 as our formula for change, we have the tools to put any change into place and to sustain it for as long as we desire.

Appendix A

Commitment to Action: I_2E_2

What are you intending to change for yourself, your team, patients and families?

Vision: (In present tense and concrete terms as experienced by others.)

_____

_____

_____

_____

Inspiration: (Who else may share your vision? How might you inspire others to support your vision?)

_____

_____

_____

_____

Infrastructure: (What changes in your daily practice would increase the likelihood that this vision could live? What are the implications for roles, rituals, systems, standards, norms, and your practice?)

_____

_____

_____

_____

Education: (What knowledge and skill building is needed for yourself and others to initiate and sustain the desired vision?)

_____

_____

_____

_____

Evidence: (How will you demonstrate or measure a persistent focus on your vision, as well as the actual impact and outcomes?)

_____

_____

_____

_____

Appendix B

The Gantt chart on the next page shows the first year of an Relationship-Based Care implementation using I_2E_2. While transformational change of this magnitude is always unique to each organization, this sample demonstrates the cyclical nature of I_2E_2. As one round of Evidence is completed, it fuels the next inspiration.

A more detailed Gantt chart, showing program details by week, over the span of three years is available by calling our office at 800.728.7766 or 952.854.9015.

RBC Implementation	Year 1 Month 1	Year 1 Month 2	Year 1 Month 3	Year 1 Month 4	Year 1 Month 5	Year 1 Month 6	Year 1 Month 7	Year 1 Month 8	Year 1 Month 9	Year 1 Month 10	Year 1 Month 11	Year 1 Month 12
Inspiration												
Relationship-Based Care (RBC) Workshop			X		X		X					
Reigniting the Spirit of Caring (RSC)									X (Lic.)			
Unit Practice & Results Council Presentations										Wave II		
Infrastructure												
Design	X		X									
On-site Consultation		X				X						X
Results Council		X				X						X
Work Complexity Assessment												
Unit Practice:												
· Wave I					X	X						X
· Wave II												X
· Wave III												
Competency									?			
Caring Model											Implementation Wave II	
Education												
RBC Leader Practicum	X				X							
Leading an Empowered Organization (LEO)	X											
· Overview	X							X				
· Shot in the Arm								X		X		
LEO Practicum												
RSC Practicum												
Leadership at the Point of Care (LPC)												
LPC Practicum												
Leadership Effectiveness Analysis												
Human Dynamics												
Workshops												
Evidence												
Outcome Measurement			X									
Environmental Study		Wave I or households										

References

Creative Health Care Management. (2003). *Leading an empowered organization: Participant manual.* Minneapolis, MN: CHCM.

Cooperrider, D., and Srivastva, S. (1987). Appreciative inquiry in organizational life. *Research in Organizational Change and Development,* 1, 129-169.

Covey, S. (2004). The 7 habits of highly effective people. New York: Free Press

Greenleaf, R., & Spears, L. (2002). *Servant leadership: A journey into the nature of legitimate power and greatness.* Mahwah, NJ: Paulist Press.

Koloroutis, M., (ed). (2004). *Relationship-based care: A model for transforming practice.* Minneapolis, MN: CHCM.

Morris, T. (1998). *If aristotle ran general motors: The new soul of business.* New York.

Peavy, F. (2003). *Strategic questioning: An experiment in communication of the second kind. San Francisco, CA: Grabgrass, http://crabgrass.org/site/strategic_1.html*

Porter-O'Grady, T., & Malloch, K. (2002). *Quantum leadership.* Gaithersburg, MD: Aspen Publishers.

Redfield Jamison, K. (2005). *Exuberance: The passion for life.* London: Vintage.

Senge, P., Kleiner, A., Roberts, C., and Ross, R. (1994). *The fifth discipline fieldbook.* New York: Doubleday/Currency.

Weinberg. D. (2004). *Code green: Money-driven hospitals and the dismantling of nursing,* Ithaca, NY: Cornell University Press.

Williamson, M. (1996). *A return to love: Reflections on the principles of a course in miracles. New York:* Harper Paperbacks.

Additional Resources:

Allen, D. E., Bockenhauer, B., Egan, C., & Kinnaird, L. (2004). Relating outcomes to excellent nursing practice. *Journal of Nursing Administration,* 36(3), 140-146.

Cameron, K. S., & Quinn, R. E. (1999). *Diagnosing and changing organizational culture.* Reading, PA: Addison-Wesley.

Capuano, T., Bokovoy, J., Halkins, D., & Hitchings, K. (2004). Work flow analysis: Eliminating non-value added work. *Journal of Nursing Administration,* 34(5), 246-256.

Cashman, K. (1998). *Leadership from the inside out.* Hoboken, NJ: John Wiley and Sons.

Gerteis, M., Edgman-Levitan, S., & Daley, T.L. (1993). *Through the patient's eyes.* San Francisco: Jossey-Bass.

Haase-Herrick, K. (2004). Letter from the leadership. *Voice of nursing leadership,* 2(5), 1, 10.

Henry, L. G., & Henry, J. G. (1999). *Reclaiming soul in health care.* Chicago: Health Forum.